A JOYFUL CALLING

*Finding Musical and Spiritual
Fulfillment in the Church Choir*

JAMES HILL

Published by Rocker Trail Publishing
e-mail: jhhill3@cox.net

ISBN: 979-8-9855868-0-0 Paperback
ISBN: 979-8-9855868-1-7 eBook
ISBN: 979-8-9855868-2-4 Hardcover
ISBN: 979-8-9855868-3-1 Audio Book

Table of Contents

Figures and Tables

Introduction

I've written this book for people who love music, who love to sing and play their instrument, and who want to grow in their faith. Whether you are new to the church choir or are an experienced chorister, I hope you find insights, suggestions, and inspiration that help make your choir experience more enjoyable and meaningful. Serving in the church choir is a calling. It is an endeavor unique from other vocations. Music, scripture, faith, and fellowship

James Hill

come together in a wonderful way, giving joy and inspiration to people in need, offering hope and consolation mixed with beautiful music. It is my earnest wish that these pages help you discover and cultivate the true benefits, some obvious and others opaque, which can be yours by serving in the church choir.

I have not written a "How to" book on the church choir or tried to delve into the intricacies of music theory, theology, and the like. Instead, I've focused on how being in the choir can change your life for the better, how you can express your love of music while growing in faith and purpose. As a singer and guitarist in my church choir for the past twenty years, the insights and opinions I've expressed are based on my day-to-day experiences and observations. Additionally, I am so honored to include the perspectives and suggestions from a niche group of supremely talented and experienced singers, musicians, pastors, and educators from various choirs, skillsets, and religious denominations. Below is a brief summary of some of the key topics covered in this book:

- Answering the call to serve, singing, and playing for a faith-based purpose
- Discovering worship music, rehearsals, singing, and playing in church
- Getting your instrument/gear prepared to play, and singing/playing with choir members
- Directing, blending with choir, handling nervousness, listening, finding a style
- Benefits of the choir, improving spiritual, physical, and mental health, making new friends
- Growing the Children's/Youth Choir, auditions, managing the class
- Events outside of church, including weddings, funerals, caroling, senior citizen concerts
- Appendices of favorite worship music, sample mission statement, and other helpful choir information
- And much more...

INTRODUCTION

If you love music, if you love to sing and play, if you want to grow spiritually, and add more purpose and meaning in your life, then the church choir is for you. I hope this book encourages you on your journey, offers intriguing ideas and viewpoints to consider, and helps you get the very best out of your choir experience.

CHAPTER 1

You Are Called! Will You Answer?

And passing by the Sea of Galilee, he saw Simon and Andrew,
his brother, casting their nets into the sea (for they were
fishermen). And Jesus said to them: Come after me, I will
make you to become fishers of men. —Mark 1:17

Finding Your Way to Church Ministry

If you are reading this book, then I believe you are being called to serve in the church choir. And if you are already serving, then you are being called to expand your choir involvement and contribution. Here's the question: Will you answer the call?

If you are a singer, musician, choir director, audio/video person, or just a music lover, the choir is the ideal place for you to share your talents. Here you can serve God and strengthen your faith by doing what you love to do anyway: singing and playing music!

Perhaps you've been attending church your whole life but never thought of joining the choir. Maybe you've been away from church for years, have found your way back, and believe that joining the choir might be fun. Or, perhaps you are a trained vocalist or musician, but never thought of joining a church choir until now. Whatever your religious or musical background, if you are hearing that inner voice prompting you to join the church choir, then answer the call, and say, "Yes!" Come and contribute your musical talents, be they large or small, to this unique endeavor, a calling larger than yourself. When you join and contribute your skills, you'll discover a community of believers who blend faith and music into a multi-faceted chorus that will enrich your life.

You will meet good people from all walks of life, vocations, talents, and perspectives—some who are new to the choir, and others who have belonged to church choirs all of their lives. You will meet people who have been dedicated to their faith their whole life, while some are just beginning their spiritual journey, and still others will have come back to church after having taken a detour. By joining this diverse group of individuals committed to a common purpose, you'll become a part of this rich tapestry of people committed to service, faith, and music.

How I Joined the Music Ministry

Everyone who joins the church choir has their story about how they came to serve. For me, I never considered being part of the church choir until I reached my forties. Coming from a musical family, I had always loved music. Back in the 1960s and '70s, our record player and radio was always on at home. My father, Monte, still plays the violin and my sister, Dina, the piano, and both are wonderful singers and musicians. Although my mother, Apfinia, did not play an instrument herself, she too loved music and wisely understood that it was a good thing for my sister and me, so she encouraged us. While she would work around the house, cleaning, doing the dishes, or relaxing in her chair, she would say, "Play me a song," and I'd grab my guitar and play a tune that I liked.

When I was done, she would still be cooking or cleaning, and she would say, "Play me another one." If you're ever wondering how to encourage your children to sing or play music, ask them to play you a song and when they're done, compliment them, and ask them to play another.

When I got married, my wife, Lory, and I lived in various communities in San Diego, California, and we attended church on a somewhat sporadic basis wherever we lived. By 2000, my family moved to Chula Vista, a suburb of San Diego, where a new church was being constructed called Mater Dei (Mother of God). In a barren field, there was a small sign proclaiming that this was the site where the future church hoped to be built. As of 2020, our church has now been completed, and it is beautiful—with large open spaces, high ceilings, beautiful artwork, wood, and stone—which all blend perfectly with the surrounding landscape. (If you wish to learn more about our church, go to the website for Mater Dei Catholic Church in Chula Vista, California, and come visit us!)

It was back before the church was completed, when my family was attending worship services that were temporarily being held in a school gymnasium, that I first noticed the choir. It appeared to consist of volunteers from the congregation. They were enjoying themselves and clearly loved singing and playing together. My son, Kenny, who was about fourteen at the time (and grew up to become a very talented musician, songwriter, and luthier), was with me. He said that he thought percussion would make an excellent addition to the choir. We found the choir director and asked her about the possibility of my son playing percussion with the choir. I was expecting a quick "Thanks, but no thanks!" but, to my surprise, she said, "Yes, that would be great!" So, by the following Sunday, my son was proudly playing percussion with our newfound choir. Later, I joined as a guitarist, and my daughter, Cherie, joined as a singer. Lory, who naturally loved seeing our children in the choir, began coming with us to church. Thus, from my son's simple act of asking to join the choir, my whole family was now coming to church together each week, which was a wonderful feeling.

If you sing or play an instrument, can direct a choir, or are experienced with audio/video technology then come join the choir. It is such a positive step with countless benefits for you and your family.

Refreshing Your Talents and Faith

A church choir is an ideal place for people to blend their love of music with faith. Perhaps you learned to sing and play as a child but left your musical passion behind as you became an adult. Maybe you attended church while growing up but drifted away as you moved out on your own. Whatever your personal story and experience, joining the choir is one of the most powerful ways to reconnect with your faith and love of music in a spiritual, positively charged environment. Prepare to be exposed to a variety of musical styles, melodies, harmonies, and arrangements. You'll grow in faith and spirit as you attend church each week.

During the rough and tumble of life, many of us lose touch with our spiritual side, question our beliefs, or even stop going to church. As we become adults and focus on things like completing our education, getting a job, raising a family, and just making our way in life, our commitment to faith can drop off our priority list. Joining a church choir can bring you back to your faith by putting you into a spiritual setting, re-igniting your love of music while surrounded by kindred spirits. Belonging to the choir gives you a mandatory reason, a commitment to attend church each week, and come prepared and ready to give your best to the choir and your church.

Less Egos, More Positive People

I've discovered my fellow choir members to be a blend of incredibly talented individuals who find inspiration and faith through the choir. Contrary to what you may have experienced playing in commercial bands, symphonies, ensembles, or other musical groups outside of the church, I think you will find that church choir involves less drama, dissent, and bruised egos than secular musical endeavors. Of course, occasional disagreements, conflicts, and differences among choir members can happen. But because the focus is on service and supporting a mission larger than ourselves, I believe that you will encounter less pettiness and self-promotion, and more kindness and understanding in your church choir than, for example, in a bar band.

Choirs are a great melting pot of people from the community, individuals from all walks of life with widely different experiences and outlooks but united in a common purpose. Some of the most accomplished, fascinating, hardworking mix of people from your community will be sitting with you each week in the choir. Becoming friends with such a diverse group of people, with all their varied backgrounds, experiences, and outlooks, has, for me, been a surprising and fascinating benefit.

A Spiritual Songbook

If you are new to the choir and are not familiar with the abundance of Christian music that exists, then be ready for a pleasant shock. Like a miner who strikes gold, you are about to unearth a vast reservoir of Christian music that will surprise and inspire you. As you become familiar with this plethora of Christian music, you'll find that many Christian songwriters take their lyrics directly from the Bible. There have been so many times that I've read a Bible passage only to realize that I have already been singing that passage in a choir song, never realizing that those lyrics came straight from the Bible. Many Christian songs are written by super-talented Christian songwriters. These songwriters have names familiar to choir members throughout the world, yet most commercial and secular audiences have never heard and will never hear of them or their music—what a shame. To see just a tiny sampling of favorite worship songs, see Appendix A.

Seeing and Hearing Beauty in Other Choirs

When I go on vacation or business travel, one of the things I like to do is attend church in the place I'm visiting. I find a church located by my hotel, and if by happenstance, the church has a choir, then so much the better. How will they sound? Where do the choir and musicians stand or sit? How are they being directed? Are they singing harmony? What instruments do they play? What is their sound system like?

There is one such church in a small town in eastern Missouri called Van Buren—a place where my family vacations from time to time. Running along the border of Van Buren is the Current River, whose flowing, clear, cold water adds beauty and movement to the wooded landscape. When in Van Buren, my family attends the St. George Mission Church, and when we were last there, some years ago, the choir consisted of a piano player and a guitar player. The piano player played steadily and well, reading the sheet music before her on the piano. The guitar player stood next to the piano and faced the congregation, singing into a solitary mic. The sound system was good and projected the voices and music through speakers mounted in the overhead ceiling.

I love the simplicity and authenticity of this type of playing by people who love music and who play without any bells and whistles, but straightforward and clear. I am sure that I never would have appreciated the charm and simplicity of a live church band had I not joined the choir. And this small choir playing in a somewhat isolated town is typical of thousands of church choirs playing all over America, all over the world. Most of these choirs are unheralded, but not unheard. They are quietly appreciated as they sing and play to the faithful in the pews.

Another thing I love about visiting other churches is seeing the incredible works of architecture, art, stained glass, sculpture, and woodwork housed within. Many churches, even modest ones, are beautiful and majestic, with a distinct personality and ambience all their own.

Figure 1-1 The Current River

Expanding Your Personal Network

One of the most enjoyable aspects of joining a choir is meeting and interacting with your fellow choir members. I think you will find that they constitute a wide, diverse set of people from all walks of life with many viewpoints and life experiences. You may find, as I did, that you meet people who share many of your same values, work in similar and dissimilar fields, love music, and add a wide circle of good people to your life. The choir is an excellent means of meeting new people and making new friends. I've also had the opportunity to play with many outstanding musicians and singers I otherwise never would have played with—from young singers who can hit beautiful high notes in clear, angelic voices, to seasoned senior citizens who sing and play with skill and maturity, and everyone in between. Senior citizens, I notice, are some of the most devoted members of church choirs. They consistently show up every week, on time, and prepared, with enthusiasm, wisdom, and commitment to service.

The Best Book You Never Read

One of the most important benefits of joining the choir is becoming more thoughtful and learned about faith. Surrounded each week by the faithful, you'll find yourself paying more attention to the readings presented during church service and the lyrics to songs. And being in church every Sunday, especially if you get there early, can give you time to read the Bible. I like to make notes in the margins next to inspiring passages that I want to remember. I especially like to annotate passages that relate to lyrics in worship songs. It intrigues me that a single phrase from the Bible can, in the hands of a talented songwriter, be transformed into a song that brings inspiration and joy to so many. Slowly over the years, my faith has grown, and, hopefully like many of you, I can trace it all back to that one moment when I said, "Yes!" to joining the choir. How will YOU respond to the call?

CHAPTER 2

A Musical Life in Church Ministry

...their sons and kinsmen arrayed in fine linen with cymbals, harps, and lyres, stood east of the altar with 120 priests who were trumpeters; and it was the duty of the trumpeters and singers to make themselves heard in unison in praise and thanksgiving to the Lord. —2 Chronicles 5:12-13

A profound musical and faith-based epiphany awaits you if you join the church choir, a possibility that you may have never considered. Here may be an unexpected avenue for you to express your commitment to both faith and your love of music in a spiritual atmosphere. An added benefit is that the congregation and choir actually want you to be there; they value your musical contributions, which will help you to feel a real sense of service. If you love to sing or play an instrument, but the idea of playing in bars, doesn't fit your current schedule or lifestyle, then consider that the venue for your musical passion and spiritual growth may be hidden in plain sight, perhaps just a few blocks from your house, at your local church.

Figure 2-1 Epiphany

Reigniting Your Musical Passion

Many of us have an old musical instrument from our childhood or high school years, collecting dust in the closet or under a bed, an adolescent relic from when we used to sing and play music. Then as we entered adulthood and focused on our educations, careers, and families, we may have neglected or even forgotten about our love for music. Joining the church choir might be just the thing to reawaken your musical passion; it can be a bold first step towards a refreshed spiritual journey.

Dina Hill, a veteran vocalist within multiple nondenominational and Catholic churches, explains her choir experience:

> "If you love to sing, then singing in the church is a great place to be. In some churches, you are singing with a small group and, as a singer, it really puts you out there. In a small choir, you may even feel some pressure each week, almost as if you were a soloist because, with a small choir, you can make a huge contribution. If you are with a larger choir, then you feel part of a larger team, with a more communal, group feeling, but with less pressure on yourself. I love singing in both."

Figure 2-2 Dina Hill

Singing and Playing Live

Gone may be the days of playing alone in your living room or only singing while in the shower or car. As part of the church choir, you can sing and play for congregations, whether modest or large in size, every week. Music in church is crucial! It adds an emotional and spiritual dimension to each service, complements the readings, and provides beauty and continuity. You have discovered the best place to sing and play!

Charles Wilson, who served in the U.S. Navy as a chaplain for 30 years, has since worked as a chaplain for the U.S. Department of Veterans Affairs and CoreCivic, providing religious programming, pastoral care, counseling, and educational support to over 2,000 persons at the Otay Mesa Detention Center in San Diego. With such experience, Charles reflects on the impact of worship music in church, both in military and civilian contexts:

"There is a tremendous benefit that spiritual/worship music can play in the church and congregation. We witness these benefits in the military, which results in an increase in regular attendance in various faith group services. The daily military life and stresses of deployments impact personnel and families, and worship music helps remind us of the bigger purposes of life. It also brings people together amid such challenges and helps the faithful to embrace the present circumstances in which they find themselves. Overall, spiritual/worship music connects them to the larger faith community outside of the military."

Figure 2-3 Charles Wilson

Depending on your church's size and how many services are offered, your choir could conceivably be heard by hundreds of people each week, which translates into thousands of people each year. Thus, you have the potential to sing and play for tens of thousands of people throughout your life and make a positive spiritual impact on their lives and on your own. What a worthy endeavor!

You are also making a positive impact on the community. If the music uplifts the congregation's spirit, then church membership may actually grow. As more people come to your church, donations can grow. With increased contributions, the church can make a more significant impact in the community by offering more support services to the needy. Thus, by joining the church choir to sing and play—doing what you love to do anyway—you can help your church positively impact the community and contribute to making your corner of the world a better place.

Getting Better All the Time

Whatever your prior musical skill level, you as a vocalist or musician will improve in the choir. If you are a singer, you will become more polished and well rounded, as your understanding of lead vocal and harmony grows. Richard Diaz, a music major at Arizona State University, has been a vocalist for various church choirs in Phoenix, Arizona, and he reinforces this perspective:

> "My singing has definitely improved from being in the church choir. My ear has become better, and I can distinguish and sing different vocal harmonies much better now than before joining the choir. Where I used to mainly hear, say, the third note over the melody, now I can hear the other harmony parts in my head, which is a great help when I'm practicing songs or singing in church."

Figure 2-4 Richard Diaz

Like Richard's experience, I have found that the more I am exposed to different styles, singers, and musicians, the more I improve.

If you are thinking about joining the choir, but are out of practice, don't let that discourage you. Invest some time and refresh your musical skills. Patrick O'Brien, a clarinetist with a Master's Degree in Performance on Clarinet from Florida State University, relates some advice. Growing up, Patrick was surrounded by family who loved to sing, but he chose a different musical path. At age thirteen, he saw a clarinet for the first time. The instrument, with its beautiful dark wood and gleaming array of keys, instantly attracted him, and he has been playing clarinet ever since. Patrick offers these suggestions to improve your playing:

"The biggest thing that you can do to build your musical skills is to consistently practice each day. Find short, one-page pieces to play. The Rose Etude books, for example, are super helpful for refining your skills. For clarinet and other woodwind instruments, there is an 'embouchure' that you form with your mouth that is very specific. If you don't practice making that form correctly, all the time, your muscles will atrophy, and you will struggle to get a good tone. Just playing for fifteen minutes each day will help build those muscles. As your playing improves, you will gain confidence. Also, do some research and find a local teacher and take some lessons, even if only for a short time."

Figure 2-5 Patrick O'Brien

A Plethora of Splendid Christian Music

As mentioned in Chapter 1, a surprising bonus in joining the choir is discovering the abundance of exceptional Christian music that exists. Much of this music is wonderfully refreshing and well written, with unexpected chord changes, descending bass lines, and beautiful melodies. As a music lover, I enjoy many genres—country, pop, jazz, bluegrass, soul, reggae, rock, and classical music—yet I never knew until I joined the choir that this enormous body of rich, soulful Christian music existed and that it combined so many musical styles.

Standing on the Shoulders of Giants

As I've become more knowledgeable about Christian music, I've begun to understand and appreciate the role that worship music has played in the American musical catalog. Consider Elvis Presley, Carl Perkins, Aretha Franklin, Sam Cooke, Whitney Houston, Marvin Gaye, Carrie Underwood, and countless other artists. You'll see the powerful influence that gospel/Christian music has had on them and their music. If you listen to Elvis singing "I Shall Not Be Moved" or "Jesus Walked That Lonesome Valley" on the "Million Dollar Quartet" Sun Sessions recordings, you will hear a unique blend of gospel, rock, bluegrass, and soul, all churned together into an irresistible musical shake, incorporating many different musical styles.

Surprising Benefits from Choir

An unexpected benefit of being in the choir is that you will develop new skills that will benefit you outside of the choir. For example, many people are afraid to speak in public. But the experience of being in a choir can give you the practice and confidence to present yourself to others with more impact, even flourish. Now when you are asked to make a toast before a crowd at a wedding reception or make a presentation at work, you will know that you can do it because you do something similar at church each week. I know in my case, I've developed better public speaking skills, which has given me more confidence in workplace, school, and social situations. Where nervousness and other forms of social anxiety can hold us back in life, the choir helps build confidence and inner fortitude.

Another bonus of being in the choir is the opportunity to network personally and professionally with a unique and diverse group of people who make up your choir and the congregation. You will meet people of all occupations, ages, ethnicities, spiritual outlooks, musical abilities, and life priorities. I've been introduced to a wonderful community of people whom I never would have otherwise met and who are now my friends.

Of all these benefits, perhaps the most profound is the opportunity to volunteer and give back to your community. On the one hand, as a member of a choir, you may feel like you are making only a small contribution to the community, since in all honesty, as volunteers, we are doing what we love to do anyway: sing and play music. But before we too easily dismiss our contributions, let us hope that by giving our best and using our talents in the choir, we are giving inspiration and joy to people through music and providing a positive message to our community.

Health Benefits of the Choir

Beyond the benefits mentioned above, being in the choir can improve your fitness, nutrition, and overall health. Because choir members and the congregation see you each week, you will want to feel and look your best. To be your best, you need to eat healthy, dress neatly (but not expensively), and pay attention to your appearance to represent yourself well at church. You may even want to increase your fitness regime. Since my father was a member of the Golden Gloves in St. Louis, I've always loved a boxing workout. So, to improve my conditioning and my stamina for choir, I joined a boxing gym. I've noticed an improvement in my aerobic fitness, breathing, and strength, which, in turn, is a great benefit when singing and playing my instrument.

I have learned that singing is much more of a physical activity than I previously thought. Singing requires you to maintain good posture, project your voice, sing "loud and proud," control your breathing, and have a strong core and diaphragm to hit and sustain high and low notes, sometimes for long periods. Also, you need to be strong aerobically, with healthy lungs and clear vocal cords. Obviously, smoking or drinking too much alcohol or other dehydrating beverages can bother your throat and vocal cords. Bad habits, combined with a lack of exercise, will stifle your musical potential and undermine your efforts in the choir. Cigarette smoking can really hurt your singing by degrading lung capacity, causing coughing, and making your voice sound raspy. Although smoking is one of the toughest habits to break, doing so will improve your voice and overall health.

Physical stamina is the hidden aspect of the choir. Some choirs stand for long periods without sitting. Are your back, feet, and knees strong enough? Can you squeeze your shoulders blades together, suck in your stomach, lift up your head, and stand with good posture? Do you have trouble sustaining notes for the required duration? Do you get out of breath? Of course, physical accommodations can be made so that choir members are comfortable, and no one is too physically taxed during choir. But consider getting a physical exam, evaluating your health, and taking steps to improve your fitness and nutrition. It will make your choir experience more fun, and you will feel better as you get healthier.

Choir Improves Your Mental Health by Reducing Stress and Anxiety

Besides encouraging our physical fitness, being in the choir can improve our mental health. There is much research showing that worry, stress, and anxiety cause us to age prematurely; they put lines on our face, reduce our immune system, and shorten our lives. According to Dale Carnegie, in his masterpiece, "How to Stop Worrying and Start Living," one of the keys to reducing worry and anxiety is finding an activity that you love to do, that absorbs and focuses your mind, and keeps you busy, so that you can, in effect, "crowd worry out of your mind." The choir serves this purpose by offering fellowship and a place where you can be busy practicing and developing your talents, doing what you love to do while growing spiritually in a positive environment.

In Winston Churchill's charming essay, "Painting as a Pastime," he recounted how, after he was unfairly fired from a high position in World War I, he sank to the depths of despair and worry. Amid this depression, he, fortunately, discovered the joy and relief afforded by painting, which gave him solace for the rest of his life, including during his time as Prime Minister during World War II. Painting, he said, focuses the eye and hand and so rests the mind. "When I get to Heaven," Churchill wrote, "I plan to spend my first million years painting." Similarly, we can use the choir to help focus our minds on positive pursuits and reduce our stress to become more mentally healthy.

Ask anyone in the choir, and they will probably tell you that being in the choir makes them feel emotionally better, spiritually stronger, less anxious, happier, and more creative. Stress reduction is also a key benefit for children and young adults who sing in the choir, as will be discussed in Chapter 7. Combine the joy of making music with the comfort and inspiration that comes from serving in church each week and being around fellow believers, and the choir can become a wonderful means for maintaining our mental and spiritual health.

During the time that this book was being written and published, the COVID-19 pandemic spread across the world. One devastating impact from this pandemic has been the mandatory shutting down of churches and church choirs across the world and the inability to rehearse, sing, and worship together through music. This cancellation of choirs has, in an instant, removed one of the most profound sources of spiritual refuge, strength, and stress relief for millions of choir members. I never imagined that anything, short of military occupation of this country by a foreign power, could cause the cancellation of choirs and churches. Yet it happened. As COVID and other similar pandemics are better understood and controlled, we can hope that choirs will again flourish and people can sing and stand together in church, following applicable health guidelines.

All the World's a Song

I've noticed that as I become more immersed and focused on music, my senses become more aware and more sensitive to sounds occurring in everyday life. The whole world begins to sound like music! When I'm in my backyard, and I watch a bird perched atop a roof or telephone pole, singing its sweet, melancholy melody, I'll wonder to myself, what key is that bird singing in? Is it C major? No, there are too many sharps and flats. A minor key? No, it sounds more like a major scale. As I'm not well versed in music theory, I quickly reach the end of my musical inquiry. But I'm sure that there has been research conducted regarding the music that birds, whales, and other creatures make and how their songs fit into our human-contrived musical scale.

I have similar experiences when I listen to the tone, pitch, and cadence of people speaking. Some people, especially singers and musicians, speak with a voice that is so pleasant—with good tone and pitch, and a defined cadence—that it almost sounds like they are singing a melody as they talk. People with melodious speaking voices have potential, I think, to be great singers. Sometimes I will compliment someone on their speaking voice, and I am often surprised to learn that they never even tried to sing or believe they can't. How many great voices has the world been denied because that person never tried to sing?

On the other hand, some people's speaking voice sounds so unpleasant or rough, that at first blush, one would think they surely could not be a good singer. But some of these same people have so much innate musical talent that they become wonderful singers even though their speaking voice seems unlikely to produce a memorable tone. Louis

Armstrong is a great example of a person who had so much musical talent that he was a great singer despite having a raspy, highly textured voice. For instance, listen to Armstrong singing "What a Wonderful World" and "Do You Know What It Means to Miss New Orleans."

I think you will find that, as you spend more time with the choir, listening to melodies and harmonies, and playing your instrument, that everyday sounds—like the crash of waves breaking on the shore, birds singing, and a lonesome train whistle reverberating down the track—begin to have a musical quality. These and other sounds become a part of life's musical chorus, playing all around us. With apologies to Shakespeare: "All the world's a song, and the people merely vocalists and musicians. They sing their songs, play their music, and each person in their time performs many parts."

Figure 2-6 Bird Chorus

Birds of a Feather, Sing and Play Together

Ever since I first joined the choir, through to this day, I have been so impressed by the musical skill, knowledge, and passion that my fellow vocalists and musicians have. You, too, will meet a diverse group of vocalists, wind players, percussionists, string players, keyboardists, and singers, some of whom have the talent to have pursued a professional life in music had they chosen that career path. Within this varied and talented group of musicians and singers, I am often humbled by my own musical limitations and shortcomings but also inspired by their strengths and enthusiasm, which influences me to try and become better.

I've gained much musical insight during my time with the choir, just listening and watching my fellow choir members. Here is one example: I used to avoid using vibrato when I sang because my ears preferred a steadier vocal sound versus the sometimes-wobbly sound vibrato produces. But through listening to other vocalists in our choir, I have come to really appreciate that extra bit of panache and flourish that vibrato brings to a song when it is done well. I've started to incorporate a measured amount of vibrato into my own singing. I should note that some choir directors prefer that vocalists just sing "straight" without adding vibrato. This is because if too much vibrato is being added by multiple vocalists at the same time, the choir as a whole may sound weird and disjointed.

As a musician in the choir, you will likely be exposed to instruments that, depending on your musical background, you may be unfamiliar with. You may find yourself among trombones, trumpets, flutes, clarinets, violins, drums, tambourines, ukuleles, and cajóns, just to name a few. Your choir director will strive to find the right balance within this diverse musical group, strategically determining who plays what, when, and where. Prepare to have your musical landscape enlarged with this cornucopia of different instruments, vocalists, and musicians.

> *So when they all sounded together, both with trumpets and voice and cymbals, and organs, and with diverse kind of musical instruments, and lifted up their voice on high.* —2 Chronicles 5:13

Being a Choir Director

A quick note on choral job titles used in this book. Church choir music directors, coordinators, and worship music leaders have different functions and job titles depending on how they are organized— but for simplicity's sake in this book, I refer to the person who coordinates, manages, directs, and stands in front and leads the choir all under one generic title of "choir director." In reality, this term is not always accurate and is an oversimplification because church choirs often consist of multiple music leaders, directors, administrators, and coordinators with various job titles who perform tasks and functions for the choir.

There is no single path to finding one's vocation in life. The road is full of detours, U-turns, and fender benders; our best-laid plans can go awry. But if you love music and feel a desire to serve your church and grow your faith, then choosing to become a church choir director as a profession is a calling like no other.

Frances Tuminting, Director of Music at Mater Dei Catholic Church in Chula Vista, California, is a multi-talented musician and vocalist who leads our choirs with a quiet confidence. Frances summed up her music background:

"My parents loved music and were active in the church, and we would go to church together. I took piano lessons for a couple of years, starting at age eight. I loved playing the piano, practiced all the time, and just kept with it. I joined the school choir beginning in elementary school and on through college. It never occurred to me back then that my faith and love of music could eventually come together, and I would become a choir director. But looking back, I can see now that the seeds that were planted way back then were just a preparation for this calling."

The role of choir director is a unique vocation that blends faith, music, and service to others. If you decide to become a church choir director, be ready to be busy! You'll spend your time teaching and managing music, choosing music for the choir, e-mailing and texting choir members, preparing the choir for major musical events, supporting funerals and weddings, fundraising, and a host of other duties.

From a compensation perspective, although choir director salaries have increased over the years, they are not still at the level they should be. The National Association of Pastoral Musicians, a Catholic association, is a helpful resource that publishes suggested salary tables and other compensation information based on whether you have earned a Bachelor's or graduate degree in music and relevant work experience. You will be expected to play your instrument well, read music, and have leadership and organizational abilities. In terms of the working environment, you will be surrounded by people of faith who are dedicated to service, but you may feel frustrated because the church administration is often short-staffed, overworked, and operates on a limited budget.

Whether you pursue the role of choir director as a primary or secondary career, or as an unpaid volunteer, it is a genuinely unique vocation. It's a calling that puts you in a spiritual setting, surrounded by vocalists and musicians who also want to serve. You need to develop a vision for the choir with thoughtful goals so that you can influence what you want your choir to be and how it should sound. And you need to be able to translate your vision into a common purpose that choir members can understand while enabling them to express their individual talents.

A choir director needs to be flexible with the ability to compromise on certain musical and administrative issues. Asking for choir feedback on specific questions and/or a vote on appropriate items of interest is an excellent way to give the choir a voice in certain issues where they have high interest. This is not to say that all choir directors are open to accepting feedback from choir members. Especially in larger churches where a choir director may be directing and managing a large number of vocalists and musicians, and working under a tight schedule, say, for example, preparing for a Christmas service, the choir director may not have the time to change plans based on choir feedback. Choir directors who are managing large choirs often believe that they are being paid to take control, direct, and mold the choir according to their vision. Thus, they are often unwilling or unable to expend valuable rehearsal time negotiating song choices, vocal parts, or instrumentation.

An Audience for Your Original Songs

Many singers and musicians have original songs in various stages of completion that they hope to someday record and publish. If you have ambitions as a songwriter, being part of a church choir is a tremendous opportunity to play your songs to the congregation (with approval of your pastor) and possibly get them recorded and published. See Appendix D for the lyrics to a song, "The Man Upon the Cross," that I wrote about faith, hope, and redemption, which captures my favorite part of the Bible. This song will soon to be available on Amazon and other related sites.

CHAPTER 3

Preparing, Rehearsing, Directing, and Enjoying

Receive one another as Christ also hath received
you unto the honor of God. —Romans 15:7

I love playing and singing worship music with my choir. We keep the mood light and fun, and I truly enjoy rehearsing the upcoming songs for Sunday and learning any new ones. In our choir, when we rehearse, we don't put pressure on ourselves to sing and play perfectly. We make lots of mistakes and have lots of redos, but we experiment and have fun. I appreciate being with people who not only love music but are talented and there to serve.

How Much Time is Needed for a Productive Rehearsal?
The amount of time needed for rehearsal depends on your choir's skill level, how difficult any upcoming new music is, and how good the choir wants to sound. And it also depends on how much time individual choir members are willing to commit to being better vocalists and musicians.

If the choir is newly formed, more rehearsal time is needed so that people can become comfortable and in sync with each other. A new choir will likely need to rehearse at least twice a week, for a couple of hours each session. And choir members should practice at home as well. Patrick O'Brien (introduced in Chapter 2) has played extensively in orchestral settings and venues and has the following comment regarding rehearsal preparation:

> "To me, the expectation for rehearsal is that you already know your part when you get there. Rehearsal should be more about group cohesion and hearing how the choir sounds together. It's also the place to make sure everyone agrees with any musical decisions impacting the choir. Musicians should practice every day to keep their fingers active. When practicing at home, first listen to the piece all the way through while looking at the music. Understand how your part fits into the whole. Focus on your most critical parts, so that when you get to rehearsal, you are one hundred percent ready to play."

As a choir gets more in sync with each other, rehearsals can become shorter and more efficient. Many choirs rehearse only once a week and then for a few minutes right before church to get warmed up and review the songs. However, special events and unique church services such as Christmas and Easter services, musical concerts, and plays with the children's choir require more rehearsals.

99% of Choir (and Life) Is Just Showing Up

In choir, one critical quality is dependability. If you join the choir, go All In. Don't be that person who shows up late, is never prepared, or doesn't come at all. Of course, in our busy lives, there will be legitimate reasons why you might be late or absent from rehearsal and church. That's understandable and happens to everyone. But if you can't make it or are going to be late, send a text to your choir director, and let them know. Then, practice on your own and be there early next Sunday to prepare. My sister, Dina, having sung with her church choir since high school in multiple churches, has this to say on the subject:

> "If you want to sing in the choir, I think it is up to you to be there on time, with your music organized. As a singer, you need to take the initiative and be fully prepared and ready to go. You also have to be ready to improvise and wing it when the unexpected happens. Maybe several vocalists are not there, and, all of a sudden, you need to take the lead. Maybe you missed rehearsal, and there is a new song that you have not rehearsed, but now you are being counted on to sing the melody or harmony. Whatever the situation, you have to be flexible and willing to sing even when you are not fully ready. In those situations, I try to keep a positive attitude, reminding myself: 'It's not just about me.'"

Preparation and Organization by Choir Directors

For a choir to work together effectively, it needs an excellent music leader. Our church is so fortunate to have such a music leader, Frances Tuminting, (introduced in Chapter 2), who not only manages and coordinates the music ministry—which requires a huge amount of work— but is also a super-talented piano accompanist and singer in our choir. Frances plays with a natural rhythm and artistry that springs from within her and sings in a clear, pristine voice.

Among the many duties of a choir director is the task of thoughtfully choosing and preparing the music to be played and tailoring those selections to the preferences of the church and congregation. Additionally, a choir director often has to handle administrative responsibilities like sending the choir e-mail updates, scheduling upcoming events, and handling personnel and staffing issues that arise.

Dr. John Mark Harris is a pianist, composer, educator, and music director at Saint David's Episcopal Church in San Diego. He has performed in venues all over the world, both as a solo pianist and as a chamber musician. He has also composed music for film and is an acclaimed music teacher. Dr. Harris describes some of the challenges of having productive rehearsals:

> "Organization is key. Just getting all the music together for keyboard, guitars, and other instruments and then arranging it takes a lot of time and effort. Also very important is figuring out a way for all choir members and musicians to participate in the choir in a meaningful way, given their different skill levels. Some choir members will be highly trained in music, perhaps they sing in a band or community opera house. But then you'll also have novices who don't read music at all. So picking music, organizing, and arranging it in such a way that is satisfactory and appealing to the whole choir is an ongoing, challenging goal."

Figure 3-1 Dr. John Mark Harris

The choir director sets the tone for how members interact with each other and with the congregation. In setting this tone, a choir director should remember to treat choir members as unique individuals—musical collaborators who have feelings and sensitivities, people who are smart and who are there to serve. Avoid any tendency, of which, I have been told, that some conductors of orchestras can be guilty, to treat the choir members as objects, tools, or somehow less than.

Preparing to Rehearse

As mentioned above, for rehearsals to be productive, a choir director must make sure that rehearsals are well planned and organized, songs are preselected, sheet music and/or digital copies are sent to the choir, and so on. Wasting the choir's time—figuring out which songs to play during rehearsal, or being disorganized and not having the music prepared—is irritating and may cause people to drop out. Dr. Harris underscores the advantages of having regular, routine, and consistent rehearsals:

"I think it's important for the choir to have a rehearsal routine that is predictable and consistent and should be done the same way, every time. That way, the choir knows what to expect each time at rehearsal. The music should have a written arrangement, so everyone is on the same page. In our rehearsal, we'll play a song over and over until we are very comfortable with it. Then on Sunday, it's easy to do—no stress. You just can't rehearse the music once or twice and think you're ready."

There may be times during rehearsal when, for whatever reason, some choir members are struggling to sing or play their part correctly. Perhaps the bass singers keep singing the wrong notes, or the wind instruments can't seem to nail the syncopation. Whatever the issue, occasionally a small subset in the choir will be having trouble with their part despite spending a lot of time on it, while the rest of the choir is watching, bored, restless, with nothing to do. When this situation occurs, rather than wasting everyone's time, consider just dismissing the entire choir, asking them to practice on their own, and reconvene at a later time to close the issues.

Choosing the Right Music

Selecting quality music is a crucial contribution of a choir director. Great music inspires us, brings joy, and gives us something beautiful and challenging to enjoy. Throughout human history, music and art have offered healing and comfort. I'm always fascinated when ancient caves and dwellings from antiquity are discovered, sometimes thousands of years old. Although these ancient peoples were often struggling to survive, they took time to create art, leaving their paintings on cave walls, in an effort to infuse beauty and artistry into an often harsh and brutal existence. In church, great worship music inspires the congregation, uplifts the choir, and enables worshippers to proclaim the Gospel with music. Worship music can best be viewed as an extension of the Gospel—an art form that supports and enhances the message of the scriptures, readings, and sermon. Worship music must be chosen wisely.

Father Jovencio Ricafort, Pastor at Mater Dei Catholic Parish in Chula Vista, points out:

"For many in the congregation, music adds so much to their worship and faith. That is why choosing songs that support faith is so important. If the choir only chooses songs that the members know or are popular, without a liturgically fitting faith-based message, then people will not feel that spiritual experience in the music. The key purpose of the choir is to lead and encourage people to sing and praise the Lord. If the songs that are selected are only ones that the choir knows and likes to sing, then the congregation misses the opportunity to strengthen their faith and will miss that spiritual experience."

Christian music has been evolving rapidly in recent years, with a fresh influx of new music, new bands, new songwriters, and huge venues. Charles Wilson (introduced in Chapter 2) comments on the importance of choosing good music.

"One of the challenging areas in choosing great worship music is maintaining authenticity, integrity, and commitment to the ideals of our faith. There is a delicate balance of not being driven deeply into the pressures of the counter-culture that may emphasize greed, ambition, idolatry, and self-aggrandizement that is so often seen in the music industry. If there is a deep understanding of integrity to faith and creative artistry to the worship music that is presented, then the evolution of any style of faith-filled music can be tremendous and so beneficial to the people."

Guidelines for Choosing Music for the Choir

Dan Quigley, former Choir/Music Director and pianist at St. Francis de Sales Catholic Church, in Chelan, Washington, explains his thoughts regarding song selection:

"I focus on the songs' lyrics because the lyrics have special meaning for the liturgy and the readings. We are, in effect, singing the liturgy. I don't want to have a situation in the choir where prayers and readings are said, and then we have a musical 'performance' by the choir. We want to choose music and play and sing it in such a way that it fits together with the liturgy seamlessly and helps the congregation come closer to God."

Figure 3-2 Dan Quigley

Below are some principles to consider when choosing music for your choir.

Table 3-1 Principles for Choosing Choir Music

PRINCIPLES	ACTIONS
Review in advance the church readings for the coming week.	Understand the readings and themes so that you can select the right songs for church service.
Read the lyrics of the songs.	The lyrics are the most important part of the music. Find music with words that support the teachings for that day.
Fit the music to a specific part of the service.	Select songs that have the right length for the part of the service in which it will be played. For example, a song for Communion may need to be longer and may need to be repeated, since Communion can take a long time.
Choose music that is enjoyable and challenging for the choir.	Pick exceptional songs that the choir loves and that are familiar to the congregation. Don't get stuck in one style or genre. Perform a cappella occasionally to showcase the singers.

Auditions, Anyone?

Many choirs allow anyone with the desire and basic ability who wants to join the choir to do so. Question: Should auditions be held to screen potential new members? Opinions vary. For churches who choose not to hold auditions for choir, the rationale is often that the church wants to foster a welcoming culture, and if someone steps forward to serve in choir, then they should be welcomed to join. But if a church welcomes all comers without auditions, how do you know if the new singer can sing? I have not seen a situation where someone was so unskilled that they were denied entry to the choir, but I'm sure it happens. Our choir welcomes all volunteers regardless of skill level, but we do rehearse enough to ensure everyone knows their part. The culture of accepting others despite their shortcomings is a consistent theme in the Bible. It is also expressed in the song "All Are Welcome" by Marty Haugen. Still, if you feel the need to hold auditions, below are some tips to consider.

Audition Considerations

As discussed above, although many churches allow anyone to join the choir regardless of experience level, it is common for larger churches to hold auditions. Often times, in larger churches, choir members are compensated professionals, so holding auditions is not unusual and helps find highly skilled people for the choir. But for the vast majority of churches who use nonprofessional volunteer members to serve in the choir, the concern with holding auditions is that a potential member who wants to serve might be intimidated by the audition process, be afraid of being rejected, and choose to not try to join the choir at all.

If you decide to hold auditions, consider not holding an "audition" in the traditional sense, but instead presenting it more as a "place-ment" or perhaps an "informational interview." This format would entail a one-on-one informal meeting with the new choir member and the choir director without auditioning in front of the whole choir. Rather than using a definitive pass/fail musical test, which can be incredibly intimidating, try making it more like an informal evaluation meeting to determine where and how a potential choir member can fit into the choir given their skill and experience level.

There is a real benefit that comes from scheduling time to talk with prospective choir members who want to join. When you meet one-on-one, you can gauge their commitment level, discuss the choir's unique mission, set expectations, and just get to know each other. This way, both the new member and the choir director get a good sense of each other, and the new member can assess if joining the choir is something they really want to do and how they can fit in.

Helping New Choir Members Develop Skills

Once a choir director has met with and evaluated a new member's skill level, the choir director and the individual can consider if they would like to improve their skills.

A choir director can place the new member next to stronger singers or musicians to help mentor them and show them the ropes. Additionally, you can suggest that the new member take outside voice or music lessons, which will quickly enhance their abilities and make the choir even more enjoyable as they grow in their talent.

One caveat: avoid the temptation to turn choir rehearsal into a music theory class. Most volunteers just want to sing, play their instruments, and serve the church. In-depth lectures on the finer points of music theory are usually not necessary for choir, can be excruciating, and may accelerate the dropout rate.

Although I think it is rare, there could be a new member who, despite their best efforts and practice, is unable to sing or play at the competency level required in the choir. I say I think this is rare because I believe that most people who are drawn to the choir have a natural talent and love for music and, with lots of practice and guidance, can become competent and even exceptional singers and musicians. And as discussed above, most churches want to foster a culture of welcoming people to the church and the choir. But although I have not seen it myself, I am sure that there are those rare occasions when an individual may be so inexperienced and so lacking the necessary musical skills that their singing/playing hurts or undermines the choir. I have heard stories of some choir directors actually turning down the microphones of individual singers to minimize their "dissonance."

If there is a situation where an individual, through lack of musical skill and experience, is actually causing a disruption in the choir and ultimately in the church, then the choir director may need to very discreetly and diplomatically suggest some options to the individual. Perhaps this person can take private lessons to bring their skills up to the required level. Also, if, for whatever reason, improving their skill set is not likely to occur, then perhaps this individual may serve the choir in a different capacity. Maybe they could help with the audio system and setup, organize the music each week, send email and text updates of upcoming events, and/or manage the choir website and social media. If none of these areas are of interest to the choir member, they may want to consider joining another ministry within the church, which may be a better fit for their talents and desire to serve.

Avoiding Elitism

An obstacle to having an inclusive choir culture can occur if a choir, especially one composed of good friends who have been together for a long time, does not welcome new people into the choir but instead tries to maintain a "choir monopoly" composed of the same people who discourage outsiders from coming in. Although a choir may make announcements in church and in the bulletin to invite new members to join the choir, the reality can be that the existing choir members don't want to share their vocal or instrumental parts with new members. If new members try to join, they are given the cold shoulder. This occurs naturally in musical groups outside of a church, where bands are much more money and success-driven and emphasize individual "performance" (discussed in Chapter 4). But in a church choir, the joys and benefits of belonging and fellowship that come from being in the choir should be shared with everyone and not monopolized by a small clique of longstanding members. Dustin, a talented contemporary musician who has played piano and guitar in multiple different music ministries in the West, East, and Midwest, including the military chapel during his military service, reveals his experience within various choirs:

> "I've found that the atmosphere and personalities of different choirs are unique and vary from church to church. Some music ministries can be very particular and picky about how things are played. The atmosphere can almost feel a little negative. Other churches are more relaxed and open about how the music and singing should sound. Also, sometimes because the choir and musicians have played together for so long, certain choirs can almost feel like a clique. In those choirs, it's easy to feel like an outsider. In that situation, you may feel like you will never really fit in."

Thanking the Choir and Musicians

It's important for choir directors and pastors to show sincere appreciation to the choir for their service. Thank the choir early and often! Whether it's for that harmony they nailed, that beautiful flute solo, those double-stops played on the cello or violin, the quality of the audio/visual/IT system, or the singer who agreed to cantor on the spot, with little rehearsal, when no one else would. At the end of each church service, our pastor always thanks our choir, all the church ministers, and the congregation who took the time to come to church and invites everyone to give each other a round of applause. The whole congregation, including the choir and other ministers, claps. It makes everyone feel good that we collectively came to church, contributed, and had a beautiful service. Taking a few seconds to do this makes the entire church feel good and appreciated.

Working with Volunteers Versus Paid Employees

Managing choir volunteers requires a unique combination of leadership, vision, decisiveness, and a willingness to compromise. Effective choir directors know when to dig in their heels or wingtips and when to accommodate the desires of the choir. It's essential to recognize that working with volunteers is far different from supervising paid employees. Because volunteers do not typically get compensated and are not employed by the church, it is especially crucial for a choir director to treat volunteers with respect and appreciation for their service. Disrespecting them or reprimanding them unnecessarily is a sure way to discourage them and cause them to quit. A choir director needs to know which volunteers are reliable and can be trusted with important assignments, such as cantoring or showing up to a Celebration of Life, and which volunteers are less dependable. Don't give critical assignments to unreliable people, as you may be disappointed.

Choir Disagreements and Issues

Inevitably, issues and disagreements in the choir will arise that need to be addressed. Common areas for contention include rehearsal schedules and frequency, poor attendance of certain members, disagreements about song choices, arrangements, who sings and plays what, and so on. Some choir members can form an exaggerated belief in the supremacy of their talents and skills and become pushy with their wants and opinions. There will be choir members who cause drama, sow discontent, are negative, and just cause problems. If an individual or a small group of people are causing problems in the choir, then they need to be counseled and everyone reminded of the choir's unique mission and that we are not performers, as discussed in Chapter 4.

If the mission and culture of the choir and church do not fit with certain choir members' needs and desires, and if an individual is causing a disruption to the choir and church, then the choir may not be the best fit for that person's service. I find that often the most talented singers and musicians are the most humble and dismissive of their own gifts and the easiest to work with.

Being Mentally and Spiritually Ready for Rehearsal

Because our lives are so busy, it is easy to come to rehearsal, all stressed and irritated from our day, with our mind focused elsewhere. It is helpful to take the time to be in the right spiritual frame of mind for rehearsal. Dr. John Mark Harris shares his thoughts on getting mentally ready for rehearsal:

"At rehearsal, what I notice often happens is that people just rush into the rehearsal room. Everyone's talking, musicians are fooling around on their instruments, and then all at once, everyone begins to rehearse. I've found that to have a really productive rehearsal, we need a calm, relaxed mindset before we begin. Just having a quiet, calming period, even five minutes before beginning, makes a huge difference. People sing and play much better. One of our choir members received a degree in meditation. Now before rehearsal, some choir members join her in the choir room and meditate quietly for twenty minutes before beginning rehearsal. It has really made a huge improvement in the quality of our rehearsals. If I get there and feel rushed, it's worthwhile for me to wait five minutes until I'm mentally ready and then start the warm-up exercises."

To reframe and ease into a spiritual mindset, many choirs begin with a prayer to focus on our spiritual mission and shed the day's burdens. My favorite prayers are those spoken from the heart, on the spot, by a volunteer who volunteers to lead the choir in a prayer. It is said that a family who prays together stays together. Similarly, choirs who pray together, I'm sure play better, and hopefully, stay together. As the Thessalonians, 5:11-14 reads, we should "Therefore encourage one another and build each other up."

Support from the Top

If your church and music ministry is truly blessed, as mine is, you'll have a pastor who is a strong advocate for worship music and the positive role it plays in church and for the congregation. A pastor who actively and publicly supports the choir inspires choir members to give their very best. The choir, especially the choir director, needs to have an advocate, someone who appreciates the role of the choir and backs them up when they need help and support. If the choir does not have a supportive and engaged pastor, then the choir director and choir may become disillusioned and demotivated.

A few years back, I attended a business conference in San Francisco. Taking a break for lunch, I took a walk to take in the sights of this picturesque city. The streets and sidewalks were packed with a bustling mid-day crowd. Walking along and taking it all in, I happened upon St. Patrick's Catholic Church, located on Mission Street, close to the Convention Center. Built of old red bricks, this church stands out prominently, as if refusing to be obscured by the encroaching city. I decided to try and go in, but because it was a Thursday, I expected the church to be closed. To my surprise, the door opened, and I walked in. Church was in progress, and Communion was just beginning. Taking a seat in the back, I was struck by the beautiful, multicolored stained glass, and watched as the pastor prepared Communion.

What stood out to me was that the pastor wasn't only speaking his prayers, but was singing them in a clear, strong voice. The organist, partially hidden behind a column near the altar, played well. As the pastor continued to sing, I was reminded of the old days when pastors often sang during church services, some on key with surprisingly good voices, others well-meaning but out of tune. This pastor, however, obviously loved music and sang well and joyfully for all to hear. His singing made a positive affirmation about how music enhances prayer.

Closer to home, I've also experienced our pastor's support for music within our music ministry. I recall on one night, our choir was at rehearsal practicing "To You, O God, I Lift Up My Soul," by Bob Hurd, for the first time. As we were warming up with this wonderful song and adding extra enthusiasm, punch, and volume, our pastor, Father Jovencio (whom we call "Father Ven"), came up and stood by the door to listen. When we finished the song, he said, "I was passing by and came over to listen. This song really attracts me. It's a really great song!" His words brought smiles from the choir, as we felt proud that our pastor had taken the time to listen and sincerely compliment us. It is amazing how much a compliment from the pastor means to the choir!

Is Reading Music Required for Choir?

Many people believe that it is necessary to be able to read music in order to join the choir, but this is often not the case. In our choir, for example, there are many talented singers who don't read music, but that does not slow down rehearsals or cause any significant issues. Choirs are often composed of people who love music, who love to sing, and who have an excellent ear for music. Even without knowing how to read music, oftentimes, choir members, under the direction of a good choir director, can pick up melodies and harmonies just by listening, recording their vocal parts on an audio recorder, attending rehearsals, and practicing on their own.

But while the ability to read music isn't mandatory, it does give a singer and musician a significant advantage in understanding music and makes the process of learning songs and singing harmony that much easier. If you don't read music but want to learn how, many excellent online tutorials are available on the Internet and YouTube to help you improve. Studying just thirty minutes or less each week will go a long way in helping you to improve.

Teaching New Songs

Each choir and choir director has their own approach to teaching new songs. I'll describe how new songs are taught in my choir. We are currently so fortunate to be led by wonderful directors who are so dedicated and generous with their talent and spirit.

The process of teaching a new song begins with our choir members receiving a link to the song via e-mail. Frances Tuminting, (introduced in Chapter 2) who leads our music ministry and is a soulful pianist and vocalist, sends a link to the song in advance of our rehearsal so that everyone has the opportunity to review the song. At rehearsal, music books are handed out. If a new choir member stares at the music and says, as they sometimes do, "I don't know how to read music," one of our choir directors will invariably respond, "Just look at the music and follow the 'dots' (the dots being the notes). Raise the pitch of your voice when the dots go up and lower the pitch when the dots go down." Music theory simplified!

To teach the choir new songs, Frances typically plays and sings the song once or twice by herself, so that the choir can hear how the song sounds and get the melody ingrained in their minds. She may play the audio of the song on her tablet so we all can hear how the song should sound. As she plays the piano, she purposely plays in a manner that strongly emphasizes and isolates the melody so that it comes through clear, distinct, and becomes memorable. Frances, who sings harmony skillfully and naturally, points out that:

> "Hearing the melody distinctly is more crucial than hearing the harmony because if the congregation can hear the melody clearly, then they will sing with the choir, which is our goal and is so wonderful to hear. Although our choir is very skilled at multi-part harmonies and we love to sing parts, we try to project a strong melody so that the congregation can follow and not get lost in the harmony."

As Frances plays the new song, Blessie Prudente, one of our choir directors, follows the sheet music and listens carefully to the new song. Blessie sings the melody with the choir, going over each verse line by line, stopping and correcting, redoing specific lines, and re-checking our timing until each phrase is learned well. Blessie smiles as she leads, keeping time with her hands, enunciating the words with her mouth, reacting to musical cues and direction from Frances. Frances and Blessie work as a team and are quick to address any choir issues and often stop mid-measure to correct intonation, poor pronunciation, or problems with timing. Once a song has been rehearsed and learned, then the musical introductions and endings are nailed down so that the musicians start and end together. With such experienced musical leaders, our choir can learn a new song, including the harmonies and instrumentals, in twenty to thirty minutes, which is always amazing to me.

Blessie loves directing the choir, and it shows. Blessie says about directing the choir:

> "I love to see the choir members really enjoying themselves, having a good time, and maintaining an atmosphere of fun in rehearsal as they serve. I love to see them so proud and dedicated to the music ministry."

Blessie is one of those vocalists who, because of her natural talent and years of singing harmony with her family and friends, has developed such a great musical ear that—even with a brand new song, and even without any sheet music—she can hear four-part harmonies in her mind, and can sing any harmony part on the spot with no music. This means that she can quickly help the choir nail any harmonies and correct any sour notes in real-time. Blessed are the harmony singers.

Hire a Good Accompanist

If you don't have a good keyboardist to accompany your choir, then hire one if possible. As mentioned above, I personally believe that having one person directing the choir and a separate person accompanying the choir on the keyboard is the most effective way to lead and give guidance to the choir. This arrangement allows the choir director to focus on directing the vocal aspects of the choir instead of trying to lead the choir while at the same time playing the keyboard. I know there are many choir directors who perform this double duty out of necessity or habit. They play accompaniment and direct the singers at the same time. But I think whenever possible, the choir should have a focused choir director giving them guidance, so that the accompanist can focus on playing. If you cannot find a keyboard accompanist, then a guitarist can accompany the choir, in the short term, but I think just barely. A keyboard is a much fuller, more versatile instrument for teaching melody, harmony, and bass lines than a guitar, and the choir really benefits from keyboard accompaniment.

No Accompanist? Use Pre-Recorded Tracks or Make Your Own

If you don't have a keyboardist or guitarist to accompany the choir, then you can buy pre-recorded tracks to play digital music to accompany the choir. My research shows a wide variety of pre-recorded Christian music is available for church choir. Select tracks arranged in the proper pitch so that the choir can comfortably sing in the appropriate range. You can download the music tracks to your phone, tablet, or laptop. Note that some pre-recorded tracks can be pricey, so make sure and research cost and stay within your budget.

If you understand audio recording and are a musician who plays multiple instruments, such as piano, guitar, bass, and drums, you can use applications such as GarageBand to record your own accompaniment using a tablet/laptop. Once you are satisfied with the recorded tracks, your choir can sing along to the created tracks. Because this accompaniment is custom-made by you for your choir, these tracks can sound amazing. Make sure and buy a quality set of audio speakers to project the music to the congregation.

Singing Harmony by Ear

Singing rises to its highest level of beauty and artistry in harmony. Voices blended closely together, creating a human chord that must be one of the most beautiful sounds in all the universe. As much as I love to hear harmony, I regret to say that I am not a strong harmony singer. If I have the sheet music to a song, study the harmony notes, and practice, I can decently sing my harmony part and I do enjoy it. But there is an extraordinary type of singer who stands apart from others. These are the people who can sing harmony by "ear," by which I mean they can sing harmony in the moment, in real-time, without looking at sheet music, and only by knowing how the melody goes. These talented individuals have developed their musical ear to such an exceptional degree that whenever they memorize a melody, they can then immediately sing harmony lines that fit perfectly with the melody. Again, the astonishing thing is not that a person can sing harmony—which is a laudable skill in itself—but that a person can do so without using sheet music and within minutes of learning the melody.

How the mind creates harmony notes is a fascinating mystery worthy of in-depth study, outside the scope of this book. One can envision that at the fundamental level, the ear hears a melody and conveys it to the brain, where the melody's pattern is absorbed and processed. The brain mentally transcribes harmony notes to fit in the same key and musical structure as the melody line. The brain then transmits this harmonic code to the vocal cords where harmony notes can then be sung. But the harmony singer's work is not yet done. As the harmony singer sings, the ears, brain, and vocal cords—like a car's navigation unit—continue to analyze, process, and re-direct the harmony notes against the melody line, adjusting notes as they go, raising and lowering pitch in lockstep with the melody, creating a human chord.

This gift for creating harmony by ear on the spot is not limited to singers but also applies to musicians. Certain very gifted musicians, my father being one of them, can play harmony on their instrument on the spot once they know the melody. So for example, if you sing to my father a song, one that he has never heard before, like I often do, he can quickly grasp the melody, then add violin harmony to the melody as you sing, including harmonic runs and fills—not just replicating the melody line, but adding harmonic notes to complement the melody. This spontaneity and facility that certain singers and musicians have to create music that is counterposed to the melody, and that enhances the overall sound of the music in real-time without sheet music, is a wonder to hear and behold. Often, the singers and musicians who can do this are not able to explain easily how they are able to do it and are humble about their great musical gifts.

But how is it that some people have this talent for singing and playing harmony and others do not? My own belief is that certain people are born with and inherit this talent from their parents and grandparents. And if these very fortunate souls cultivate these inherited gifts by singing and playing an instrument, then, as their artistic skills grow, they reap a truly remarkable musical harvest. As previously mentioned, Blessie Prudente is a preeminent harmony singer in our choir and says the following regarding harmony singing:

"I believe that the ability to sing harmony by ear is a gift from God." (pointing her fingers to Heaven). "Many people can look at sheet music and figure out the harmony parts and sing the notes as written. But I believe to be able to sing harmony without needing to see any written notes is a gift that we are given so that we can share music with the congregation. I also notice that the ability to sing harmony tends to run in families, and usually, you'll find that parents, brothers, and sisters are also harmony singers."

Added to Blessie's point about families singing harmony, one of the Beach Boys, a prolific harmony band, said that the best harmonies come from singers who are related to each other. This is because people who are related to each other have voices that inherently sound similar to each other and, thus, blend really well together.

Teaching Harmony to Choir

Any detailed suggestions for learning to sing harmony would constitute a book in itself and the Internet is full of resources and teaching videos. Learning to sing harmony can take years, and success depends on a person's skill level, talent, and dedication. But there are a few general tried-and-true approaches to implement. Here is the process that I've observed in my choir for teaching harmony using sheet music. Our choir director sings the various melody and harmony parts out loud, with the piano playing the melody and harmony accompaniment at the same time. Our choir director will sing the bass, tenor, alto, and soprano parts, one at a time, so everyone hears how their individual parts should sound. Then the choir, who have been listening and following along with the sheet music, practice singing the various harmony parts. The choir repeats their individual parts until they learn them well and can sing all four parts together. Our choir director listens closely and stops and corrects individuals on the spot when she hears sour notes.

A good approach for teaching harmony to the choir is to identify the strongest singers in your choir, the ones with the best ears for music, and teach the harmony parts to them. Then, once they master their parts, have them teach the harmony parts to the other choir members.

Another approach is to divide the choir into two separate groups, with one group singing harmony and the other group singing melody.

Then, after each separate group masters their part, bring the two groups together to sing the melody and harmony parts as one choir.

A Smorgasbord of Instruments and Musicians

If you are a musician, then playing with choir musicians will be an ear-opening experience that will likely strengthen your overall musicianship. Exposure to diverse instruments and musicians will help you sing and play better because you'll continually hear unique sounds, unfamiliar rhythms, and previously unconsidered techniques. Your choir may have diverse multiple instruments, including violin, cello, organ, flute, saxophone, trombone, standup bass, etc. On the other hand, you may play in a small, more basic choir, consisting of just piano, guitar, and the vocalists.

As you become more acquainted with the various instruments played in your choir, you'll notice striking differences in instruments. For example, you'll hear how the wind and brass musicians use their breath in varying ways to produce a wonderful and distinctive vibrato. And if you're like me, you'll marvel at how much emotion the upright bass, violin, and cello can generate in the hands of great players as they draw their bows across the strings, again using powerful vibrato to create rich, soulful sounds that reverberate throughout the church. And singers with a strong sense of rhythm and movement can make even the humble tambourine sound terrific by adding that "jingle jangle" percussive sound. This smorgasbord of instruments will expand your musical perspective and open your mind to a wider field of sound.

Recording Your Choir

One device that has brought me much joy is my digital recorder, which I use to record songs during our rehearsals and at church. I've also been able to capture many live jams with family and friends. Listening to recordings of our choir rehearsals allows me to hear and analyze how we sound together. I can also hear where I need to individually improve and grow as a musician because I can hear where I sounded good and where I missed the mark. It also helps me to avoid falling into a musical rut playing the same predictable rhythms, the same melodies, and the same old riffs over and over. Many times, in my mind, I have imagined that I played a particular song or measure well, only to hear the playback from my digital recorder, and realize that there was a big difference between how I thought I sounded and how I really sounded. These recordings are not intended for anyone else to hear but me, and it is humbling to hear my shortcomings—where I sped up or slowed down, where I got too loud or soft, where I played the wrong part—and where I played well. Recording my sound allows me to hear and correct my issues, and I think you will find recording yourself is helpful and enjoyable.

There are a wide variety of digital recorders to purchase. I use the Zoom H2n Handy audio recorder because it is super portable, sounds great, is easy to use, and can be played through my car speakers while I drive to and from work. I also use the Zoom Q2n-4K video recorder for filming jams and concerts, with high-quality audio. A higher-end Zoom audio recorder that I have never tried but that I understand produces amazing results is the Zoom H6. One member of our choir uses a TASCAM digital audio recorder. There are many affordable model recorders to choose from, so start by doing your research and reading reviews to find a recorder that meets your needs and budget. For convenience, many people just use their cell phones to record music. However, while the quality of cell phone audio recording is becoming really good, it still cannot match the high quality of a dedicated digital recorder.

CHAPTER 4

Singing and Playing in Church

*You are the light of the world. A city set on a hill cannot be
hid. Nor do men light a lamp and put it under a bushel, but on
a stand, and it gives a light to all the house. Let your light so
shine before men, that they may see your good works and give
glory to your Father who is in Heaven. —Matthew 5:14-16*

Singing and playing music in church is an experience like no other.
Faith and love of music come together in a unique and meaningful way, distinct from all other musical endeavors. The readings,
the music, and prayers all blend together with a spiritual theme and
purpose. It is art, but it is art combined with faith and service. I look
forward to playing with my choir every Sunday and regret those times
when I have to miss because of some conflict. When you join the choir,
you become part of a long, rich legacy of Christians who, for thousands
of years, have sung songs, played instruments, and come to church to
express their faith, love of music, and desire to serve. You'll feel a connection to your choral brothers and sisters from generations past, who
sang and played before you, on whose shoulders you now stand, and

who proclaimed their faith through music. It is a unique, spiritual collaboration, and a fraternal association like no other. The rewards are rich, and in time, I believe that you will feel that you are not the one giving, but the one receiving gifts and rewards.

Figure 4-1 Faith and Music

Not a Performance

When you play or sing in the church choir, it should not be considered a "performance." Performance is what an entertainer does when they put on a show for the enjoyment and entertainment of an audience. Father Jovencio Ricafort (introduced in Chapter 3), gives his perspective:

"Faith and worship should always be the focus of your participation in the church choir. We are celebrating the service, and the choir and musicians in the music ministry have gifts to share. The choir should never be about personal wants and preferences."

As a church choir member, you are serving God, using whatever musical talents you have been given for a faith-based purpose. And because you're not performing for others, you can, perhaps for the first time in your musical life, ignore that inner competitive desire to out-sing or out-play another artist, and instead, just focus on being the best servant you can be.

Check Your Ego at the Door

In the commercial world, the music business is competitive; singers and musicians are judged against each other, and people try to outperform each other. But competition and performance are not the goals of a church choir. Here, you can put away those competitive tendencies and give your ego a vacation. As discussed above, you are not "performing" and trying to outshine the other singers or musicians. Rather, you are quashing your individual needs and desires; you are putting the goals and the mission of the choir first and foremost. It is a liberating feeling.

Dan Quigley (introduced in Chapter 3) has served as a choir director and has an extraordinary virtuosity on the piano encompassing many styles. He is also a songwriter and vocalist, at ease singing lead or adding harmony by ear. Dan sums up how he views the collective goals of the choir:

"As the keyboardist and music director, I want our choir to seem invisible to the congregation, so people can really commune and be transcendent with God. I want the choir and music to stay out of the way. We want to make beautiful music and allow people to pray and reflect on God. The music being played should help them reach that place, which is why I try to avoid making mistakes during church services. A mistake, if noticed, interrupts those contemplative moments."

While putting the choir ahead of our own wants and desires is the goal, despite best efforts, inflated egos, lost tempers, pride, self-importance, and a persistent competitive spirit can still breed and fester. Disagreements on things such as what music to play, how it should be played, or who should play which part, can undermine our shared goal of service and faith. Remembering that, as a choir member, I am not there for myself, but for a higher purpose, helps me maintain perspective. If you find yourself dwelling on some petty disagreement or if you become irritated about some minor issue, it's beneficial to remember the words of Matthew 5:4: "Blessed are the meek, for they shall possess the Earth." Also, from Matthew 5:9, "Blessed are the peacemakers, for they shall be called the children of God."

Managing Nervousness

Singing and playing in church for the first time can be intimidating. You may initially feel overly self-conscious, even jittery. Added to this, most church choirs are positioned directly in front of the entire congregation, so if you do feel nervous, you will be nervous in front of many people. While more experienced choir members may appear entirely relaxed and natural in front of an audience, even the most experienced and talented artists get nervous.

Henry Poblete, an accomplished choir flute player, who grew up in Manila (Philippines), and then later played flute in the United States Air Force band for twenty years, says:

"When I was young, I sometimes would get nervous, especially if I didn't practice. But if you practice your part and learn the piece well, there is no reason to be nervous. Teach your mind to relax and, most importantly, enjoy what you're playing, and the nervousness will go away."

Patrick O'Brien (introduced in Chapter 2), says regarding nervousness:

"The ability to play for an audience is a different skill set than playing your instrument at home or with your other musicians during rehearsal. One way to become more comfortable playing for an audience is to play for your friends and family. This can be difficult to do on a regular basis because it can be hard to find people to come and listen to you play. But the more people that you can play for, the more comfortable you will become, and the less nervous you will be when you play for an audience."

Another talented musician, Bob Diaz, a flamenco guitarist, former music teacher, and lifelong musical artist, offers this advice:

"To reduce your nervousness and to play and sing well, you have to over-prepare. You have to practice the songs many more times than you think you should. Make sure to practice right before you play, so your voice and fingers are warmed up and be 100% ready. If you don't practice enough and don't warm up, you may make mistakes."

You may believe that self-consciousness and nervousness are embedded in your DNA and will always be with you, and you may be right. But because of your experience in the choir, I'm sure that you will eventually become more comfortable singing and playing in front of crowds. You'll learn to reframe your nervousness, which in reality is just your body creating adrenaline and endorphins, pumping blood to your body, and in short, giving you a supercharged energy cocktail that you need to excel. So, accept that you get nervous, learn to anticipate that exciting sensation, and repurpose that nervous energy so that you can hit your high notes and play your solo, with an extra bit of panache.

Figure 4-2 Bob Diaz

A Most Reverent Venue

A church is an extraordinary place to sing and play music. It is a high privilege and honor to be a part of the choir and take your place with your fellow choir members in this unique setting. An altar is a reverent place, a unique vantage point to view and participate in the service. But being there each week, month after month, year after year, it's easy to become desensitized, even complacent. The choir is often positioned in front of the congregation, where everyone can see us. So as much as possible we should avoid daydreaming, checking our phone, chatting, and, especially, napping.

Dustin, a guitarist, and vocalist in various churches, recalls how he is often surprised when, while a pastor is preparing communion and praying, he sees band members making small talk among themselves and not paying attention in the service.

Richard Diaz, a vocalist at a variety of churches in Phoenix, points out that concentrating on the liturgy while at the same getting prepared to sing the responsorial or cantor parts can be challenging:

> "Sometimes, it's difficult to be focused on the service and preparing to sing. I'm listening to the readings, but at the same time, I'm thinking about what I am going to sing in the Responsorial hymn. My eyesight is not as good as it used to be, so I really need to think about the lyrics and focus on what I will sing. I concentrate on the words so I can do it right and not mess up. But the good Lord always helps me and puts my eyes, the words, and my voice just where they need to be."

While the choir is often located in front of the congregation, it's not unusual for the choir to be positioned away from the people, more to the side of the church or in the back of the church in the choir loft. The Mission Basilica San Diego de Alcalá was founded in 1769, and if you visit San Diego, you need to visit this beautiful and historic church, one of many missions founded by the Spanish in California. At "The Mission," the choir is sometimes located at the rear, up in the rafters where people can hear but not see them. Being out of sight of the congregation can sometimes be a nice break because you can focus exclusively on your singing and playing. But I prefer being in front of the church and being able to see the congregation. I feel more connected and a part of the service, and I enjoy looking out at the people and feeling part of the mix.

Figure 4-3 The Mission Basilica San Diego de Alcalá

Figure 4-4 Choir Loft Steps

I recall how one church volunteer would often close his eyes, in what I first supposed was prayer. But he then began to actually nod off during the service. His low, rumbling snore, sounding like a muted buzz saw, reverberated quietly but steadily. As someone who gets sleepy easily myself, I sympathize with how hard it can be to stay awake when you get that drowsy feeling. One Sunday, this member stood up during the entire service—perhaps to fight off sleep—leaning against a large door in the gymnasium where the service was taking place. Soon I heard that familiar, unmistakable rumble permeate our choir area. I looked over, and to my astonishment, he had dozed off despite being upright. I was amused and impressed by his remarkable ability to sleep while standing, and I turned back to my music. A few seconds later, a loud crash boomed as the door he was leaning against opened, and he tumbled backward onto the pavement, with the door automatically slamming behind him. It happened so fast that I don't think the congregation saw what happened. During a pause in our playing, I went outside to check on him. I found him hobbling along the pavement, rubbing his leg. I asked if he was okay, and he said by way of explanation, "Yes, I was standing there and my knee for some reason gave way!" A gentle reminder to avoid sleeping in church.

For Musicians: Sit or Stand?

In deciding whether to take a bath or a shower, Winston Churchill once said: "Why stand when you can sit?" While most choirs stand while singing, musicians can often choose whether to stand or sit while playing. This simple choice can make a big difference in how well one connects with the congregation, interacts with the choir, and even how well you play your instrument. Both positions have their plusses and minuses. Standing while playing your instrument creates a powerful feeling of connection with the music and the congregation. For a lot of musicians, it feels really good and natural to stand while playing; you can move with the music, and this energized feeling translates, I'm sure, into more joyful playing.

On the other hand, sitting down can be a more comfortable and ergonomic way to position one's hands and body on the instrument. It can be tiring to stand with your instrument for long periods, so if sitting down is more comfortable, this may cause you to play better. But if you prefer to stand while playing, and if you play a big instrument like a guitar or electric bass, consider investing in strap locks to avoid dropping your instrument, as I'll describe in Chapter 5.

Music Stands

Unless you have memorized your music, you'll want to use a music stand to hold your sheet music, tablet, cell phone, or another device. As I'll also discuss in Chapter 5, spend a little extra money to purchase a quality stand, not the flimsy kind that collapses unexpectedly under the weight of a block of rosin or guitar pick. Note that a downside to a music stand is that it creates a physical/psychological barrier between you and the congregation, in the same way that the body of a piano creates a barrier between the pianist and the congregation. Although it may seem a small thing, this barrier creates a separation between the congregation and the choir.

To help minimize this issue, challenge yourself to memorize, at the very least, the songs that your choir plays at every church service and that are in regular rotation. When you memorize music and don't need to stare at your tablet or sheet music, you'll feel free and unfettered, like surfing without a leash. If you can memorize at least the more common pieces, your enjoyment—and the overall sound—will improve as you focus more on singing and playing and less on reading notes and lyrics. Of course, it's not practical to memorize all the music; there is way too much. But it is a worthy goal to memorize the standard pieces and your favorite songs. Yes, it is scary to play without music (what if you forget and make a mistake), but it's also challenging. You will sound better as you play from your heart and soul and not be distracted by always having to stare at music.

Let There Be Light

If you use sheet music and not a device to read your music, it is crucial to make sure that you will have enough light to see your music. Imagine right before playing your part, you realize that it's too dark to read your music! This happened to me one evening while playing at a Celebration of Life. I thought I was prepared and ready; I had my reading glasses, my music organized, and my instrument tuned. But I realized after we began that the room was dimly lit, making it nearly impossible to see my music. I made it through, but now I keep a clip-on light in my gig bag for this situation. Of course, digital tablets, with good resolution, help solve this problem.

Device or Sheet Music?

As already mentioned, you'll observe some choir members using tablets, laptops, and cell phones to display their music and lyrics, while others use sheet music hard copy. There are clear advantages to using a device and these benefits are growing exponentially as tablets/laptops continue to evolve. A vast library of music is available virtually at your fingertips, and any song is only a click away. Also, from the arrangement perspective, tablets/computers offer real-time music editing, organizing, highlighting and changing measures, and, depending on your copyright license, sharing music with other choir members instantaneously. No more scurrying to the copy machine at the last minute to make copies. I use an application called "forScore" with my iPad, which has a smart keyboard and stylus pencil for making notes/ changes on my music. The iPad has enabled me to become much better organized and quickly access my library of music, create set lists without a steep learning curve. No more carrying around huge binders of music and constantly transferring hardcopy from binder to binder, repairing binder holes, and misfiling my music. Plus, in a time when musicians wonder if, in the near future, there will be enough trees in the world to even build wood instruments, digital music reduces wasted paper and hopefully saves trees.

Arlene Belenzo is a volunteer choir director of the children's/youth choir at Mater Dei Catholic Church in Chula Vista, where as part of her ministry, she teaches faith and music to children and young adults. Arlene offers her experience using a tablet for the choir:

"I was so scared at first to change from paper to a tablet. But I have a friend, a choir director at another church, and she encouraged me to try a tablet. So I did, and now using an iPad has become second nature. In fact, it's funny because when I forget my tablet at home, and I have to use sheet music in the choir, my fingers forget that I'm not using a digital screen, and my fingers automatically tap my choir book to navigate or change the page. I have all my music downloaded and organized on my iPad to access my music quickly. I'd never go back to only using paper."

But there can be drawbacks to relying solely on technology. These include slow or unreliable Internet connections, loss of power, technical malfunctions, and worst case, dropping and breaking the device on the day of the service/event, leaving you without any music. Hardcopy sheet music, on the other hand, if it is organized and if you remember to bring it, is relatively low risk and foolproof. Also, some people prefer the sensory experience of using hardcopy sheet music that you can actually feel, turn the pages, and hold in your hand. For me and other choir members that I talk to, using a tablet to access and organize music is the best, most convenient way to go. If you transition to a tablet, be cautious about depending entirely on one device to access your music. Consider having a backup device or have a paper copy just in case.

Come Early

Come early to church! As a vocalist, you'll want to get a good position, warm up your voice, review the songs, organize your music, make sure you have water to quench a dry throat, and so on. As a musician, you'll want to find a good place to stand or sit, get your gear/instrument plugged in and tuned, and set up your music. Most churches start precisely on time, which means that if you are scheduled for the 9:00 AM service, the service will begin at 9:00 AM sharp, with or without you. Give yourself ample time to be ready before church begins. Consistently rushing in late and looking hurried and discombobulated causes unnecessary stress and is a distraction to your choir mates. I find that getting to church early, even if just by a few minutes, is really beneficial. I use this time to get all set up, review the songs, and read the church bulletin before the service begins.

CHAPTER 5

Instruments, Tone, and Gear

Praise him with the sounding of the trumpet, praise him with the harp and lyre, praise him with timbrel and dancing, praise him with the strings and pipe, praise him with the clash of cymbals, praise him with resounding cymbals. —Psalms 150: 3-5

Musicians love to play their instruments! And playing in church may be the place, more than anywhere else, where you will truly improve and thrive as a musician and vocalist. You are playing with singers and musicians who are self-motivated to give their best, not for themselves but for a higher purpose. The environment is often exceptional. If you are in an actual church building, you may be surrounded by magnificent vaulted ceilings, open spaces, and hardwood/stone floors.

The acoustics in churches are often unmatched for quality and fullness of tone. In fact, many churches are designed to have a place set aside for the choir and musicians to sing and play—with built-in sound systems that project the music throughout the church. The choir is usually not an afterthought in church, but an integral part of its architecture, plan, and mission. But even if your church service takes place in a rented office building, it doesn't really matter. Use whatever space, instruments, and equipment that you have available, and step up and serve.

Resurrecting Your Instrument

You don't need a fancy or expensive instrument for church. Your instrument may be old, a budget model, a "beater" that has been knocking around your house for years. Don't be discouraged or embarrassed if your instrument is not an expensive, professional model. Embrace its humble nature and maximize its potential by performing simple maintenance to get it ready to play. If it's a woodwind instrument, disassemble it as needed, and swab it out until it is spotless and hygienic. Buy a supply of new reeds and other items that your instrument needs, and get it ready to play. Find a quality cleaner and polish it. Wipe away any grime and dirt until your instrument shines with pride. Often for a moderate price, you can have a local repair shop replace broken and worn-out parts. To further punch up your instrument's mojo, accessorize it by purchasing a new strap, instrument stand, shoulder rest, new case, a new bow, drumsticks or pedals—anything to spice up its cachet. Splurge and invest in accessories that project your instrument's personality. There is a challenge and then a pride that comes from taking a budget instrument—especially one you have a history with—and investing the time to transform it into an instrument worthy of taking its place with you among the finest instruments and musicians in your choir. (See Appendix D to know more about my first guitar and first music teacher.)

The same thing is true if you have a budget piano at home that you have neglected. Clean and shine it until that beautiful wood grain shows through. You may need to bring in a piano repairperson to fix broken pedals, sticking keys, tuning issues, and so on. Accessorize your piano with things like an LED piano light to illuminate your sheet music or a tablet to display your music. Buy a quality piano bench with adjustable height and a comfortable cushion. Move your piano to a place in your home where the acoustics resonate fully. Raise or open the piano top so that the full breadth of its tone and volume is proclaimed. If you have an electric keyboard, buy a good set of external speakers so that the tone is full and loud. If you're in a musical rut on your acoustic piano, try switching to the electric piano. The contrast in instruments will help you out of your rut.

A good musician can make even the cheapest instrument sound good, just as a bad musician can make the most expensive instrument sound bad. Get to know your instrument well. Listen to its tone varieties—its bass, trebles, shakes, buzzes, and rattles. Find its sweet spot for tone, volume, and action, and play there. Strive to make your instrument, however humble, sing to its full capacity and potential. So much of your sound comes from your heart, brain, and fingers, not just from your instrument's design and hardware. My cousin, Donny Diaz, an excellent, very tasteful guitarist, once told me, "No one plays an instrument as well as its owner." Prove that to be true, and squeeze every ounce of righteous tone from it. Be a virtuoso on your instrument.

Buying an Instrument

It is so convenient to buy your dream instrument online. And depending on the lack of music stores in your area, buying online might be your best option. But if you have a good music store nearby, go there first before buying online, and see if you can find your instrument there. Do your research in advance, get advice from friends, and become super knowledgeable about the instrument you want. Then, when you get to the music store, a salesperson can help you evaluate and pick the best one for you. You don't need to decide that same day on the spot, under the salesperson's eye. Go home and think about it, sleep on it, weigh your choices, and pick the perfect instrument for you. If you don't have a good music store in your area, do your research, and buy your instrument online. Online music stores offer extensive selections of quality instruments, often at competitive prices. Make sure that you understand the return policy so that if you don't like your purchase, you can return it.

Strap Locks

If you play guitar or electric bass and stand up during practice or while playing at church, consider installing strap locks. Without them, your instrument can slip off the strap and fall to the ground. Here's my experience. My friend Stacy, who loves to sing, asked the band at his wedding reception if they would let him come up on stage and sing a song together with me, to which the band agreed. I asked the guitarist if I could play his guitar, which was a beautiful blonde Fender Stratocaster, while we sang. Now, musicians know that asking to play someone else's instrument is a big deal. People don't like to loan their instruments to strangers, and rightly so. But this guitarist said, "Sure," with a smile. But before he handed me his "Strat," he became more serious and said "Do me a favor. This is a '57 Strat. It's super valuable. PLEASE don't drop it." I felt the real concern that he had and understood that he was trusting me, a stranger, to take care of his instrument. I told him I would be very careful.

Then, Stacy and I launched into one of our favorite tunes, which we sang together all the time, "I Saw Her Standing There." The band's bass player and drummer joined in, their guitar player standing off to the side. It was so fun, and everyone was dancing.

Then it happened. Suddenly and quickly, before I had time to react, the guitar strap slipped off the strap button, and this '50s icon was hurtling to the floor. With nanoseconds to react, I caught the guitar just before it could crash to the floor. I recovered my composure, reattached the strap, and kept playing. People dancing were oblivious to what had happened. Only its terrified owner and I understood how a near-tragedy was averted.

My advice: If you play standing up, consider having strap locks installed on your instrument. Either do it yourself or have a shop do it. And while some players believe that strap locks detract from the originality, value, and look of the guitar, what value is a broken instrument?

Electric Guitar

With its versatility and abundance of tones and styles, the electric guitar is a fantastic instrument to support Christian music. Just as a pianist plays differently on an electric piano or organ than on an acoustic piano, so a guitarist plays differently on an electric guitar than on an acoustic guitar. The electric guitar's easy-playing neck tempts you to play more aggressively, more innovatively, adding riffs and bar chords high up the neck, bending strings, etc. With an acoustic guitar, you'll often play in the first position (between the first and third frets) and play open chords. The electric guitar compels you to play at the fifth, seventh, and twelfth frets, and beyond. It's interesting how playing a different instrument can influence your mood. When I play an electric guitar, I feel the desire to learn scales to improve my solo playing, and I inevitably turn up the volume (while being careful not to annoy my fellow musicians). For me, a quality solid body guitar, with a "hard tail", i.e., no vibrato arm, exemplified by the 1976 American made Fender Stratocaster shown in Figure 5-1, is the ultimate trouble free, fun, electric guitar. A solid body guitar is generally tough and reliable, with a simple design, and so easy to play. But I also love semi-acoustic guitars like the Gibson ES-175 and the Chet Atkins Gretch shown in Figure 5-1 and the Harmony shown in Figure D-1. These guitars have a tone, richness, and a complexity that are very different from a solid body. But the disadvantage is, because semi-acoustic guitars are hollow, they are more fragile and temperamental.

Figure 5-1 Electric Guitars

Unlike the almost limitless musical potential of the electric guitar, an acoustic guitar makes a much more subdued statement. It combines simplicity and elegance to produce a truly memorable tone. An acoustic guitar, as with other stringed instruments like violin, bass, and cello is a very physical instrument to play. It's tough on your fingers, wrists, and hands, compared to the easier action of an electric guitar. On my acoustic, I prefer my string setup slightly higher so that I can dig in for rhythm, lead, and fingerpicking while avoiding buzzing strings. I pay a bit of a price for that, as it is harder on my hands and fingers. Because an acoustic guitar is mostly hollow, it's lightweight and easy to hold while standing and playing. And unlike an electric guitar, where— if your sound system or amp is not working, you'll be without any sound—you can just play an acoustic guitar louder or stand closer to a microphone, and you will probably be heard.

Electrifying Your Acoustic Guitar

I'm a proud owner of a 1973 Martin D-18 and a 1976 Martin D-35. I love them both, and I alternate playing each one, so neither gets jealous of the other. I polish their finish, clean the fretboard, change their strings, and hang them on the wall in my music room and admire their beauty. I've made one necessary alteration to both: I installed a Fishman Matrix Infinity pickup with a built-in pre-amp allowing for adjustment of volume and tone. For discussion purposes and to avoid confusion, this section refers to a pickup with a built-in pre-amp with volume and tone adjustments as an "active pickup."

Many contemporary guitar makers like Taylor, Takamine, Martin, Gibson, and Fender offer high-end versions of their guitars with active pickups already installed. But if you have an older guitar or a "budget model," you may not have any pickup installed on the guitar. This situation may be OK, depending on your circumstances in church. If you are playing in a very small church that doesn't use a PA system, amplifiers, or mixing board, then perhaps you don't need to amplify your instrument at all. There is a freedom that comes from playing "unplugged," creating music by just you and your instrument without having the sound processed and digitized by a sound system. But much more likely, you'll need to amplify your instrument. Your local instrument repair shop should have experienced craftsmen who can help you select and install your instrument's sound system. There are many different sound systems that you can have installed on your guitar to suit your individual taste. Do your research and pick one that works best for you.

Choosing a Piezo or Magnetic Pickup for Your Acoustic Instrument

As discussed, if you are playing in a larger church facility that features a mixing board, a sound person, and/or other amplified instruments, you'll need an instrument pickup. The most popular is the piezo-electric pickup (piezo), which is usually hidden from view in various locations in an acoustic instrument to amplify the sound. A piezo works by capturing the actual vibrations of the strings and the resonance of the wood on the instrument. You'll often see piezos mounted under the saddle on an acoustic guitar or on the tailpiece on a standup bass, as these locations allow the piezo to accurately project the natural, authentic sound of the instrument. The generated voltage from a piezo pick-up is so small that you will probably want a pre-amp to boost the signal, which means your piezo pickup may come with a nine-volt battery. Avoid cheap piezo pickups that will sound clacky, mid-rangy, or tend to feedback if turned up too loud. Companies like Fishman, L.R. Baggs, and K&K produce top-of-the-line pickups that consistently sound exceptional.

Instead of amplifying your acoustic instrument with a piezo, some musicians choose to use a magnetic pickup. Magnetic pickups are especially helpful when playing at louder volumes. A magnetic pickup has one or more magnet pole pieces wrapped around by a wire coil. When a string made out of a magnetic metal is struck and vibrates, the magnetic field that is created produces electric signals that you can amplify to create your sound. John Lennon famously used this pickup on his epic Epiphone EJ-160E acoustic guitar. You will commonly see a magnetic pickup mounted at the end of the instrument fingerboard by the sound hole. While some players believe that magnetic pickups rob an acoustic instrument of its natural tone and make it sound more like an electric instrument, my son, Kenny Hill, a talented musician, songwriter, and luthier, loves magnetic pickups:

"Magnetic pickups give your instrument more volume with minimal feedback. This is especially true for instruments such as an upright bass. One disadvantage to magnetic pickups is that you do lose that traditional acoustic sound. But this is not a bad thing. I have a "mag" installed on my Recording King acoustic guitar (similar to John Lennon's acoustic guitar), and it has a great, full sound, like a jazz guitar."

Do-it-yourselfers can install these pickups themselves. But before attempting it, review an instruction video online. StewMac is a great online resource for do-it-yourselfers. If you don't feel competent working on your own guitar (like I don't), find an excellent local guitar repair shop and have a professional do it.

Figure 5-2 Kenny Hill

Tube Amps

Many musicians believe that tube amps have a richer, more vibrant sound than solid-state amplifiers. I own a 1966 Fender Deluxe Reverb, which has a tone that is warm and alive, but also naturally crunchy and rumbly at louder volumes. I have to smile when I flip on the power switch and watch the jewel glow red as the amp comes to life. I feel like I'm transported back in time, jamming with my friends in the garage, our tube amps cranked to max (and neighbors annoyed!)

Many music worship leaders *prefer* the tone of tube amplifiers, with names such as Fender, Vox, and Marshall. But as splendid as these tube amps are, they can be temperamental, high-maintenance, and easy to break. Because tubes are made of glass, be extremely gentle when transporting them or setting them down. If you choose a tube amp for church, have spare tubes on hand just in case. It doesn't hurt to have a solid-state amp as a backup just in case a tube unexpectedly, inevitably, dies, or some other failure occurs. When it comes to using vintage equipment, expect the unexpected!

Solid-State Amplifiers

Solid-state amplifiers are reliable, as well as much lighter to carry than tube amps, and may incorporate onboard effects. In terms of tone, solid-state amplifiers and/or modeling pedals and processors sound so good these days that even experts have trouble distinguishing between a vintage tube amp and digital processor set to a vintage amp tone. Plus, software applications such as Guitar Rig and iGuitar are innovating how musicians shape their tone, because applications like these can emulate classic amp sounds and come loaded with varying effects such as classic flanger and delays. If you use effects, then a solid-state amp may be your best setup. Unlike pricey and temperamental tube amps, solid-state amps are affordable, reliable, and—one thing I especially love—they don't weigh a ton!

Figure 5-3 1966 Fender Deluxe Tube Amp

The Sound Person

It's been said that a lawyer who represents himself has a fool for a client. So too is a choir who mixes their own sound without having a knowledgeable sound person. One of the choir's challenges is that the choir often does not know how the vocals and instruments are sounding in the church because the choir can only hear how they sound in the area where they are standing. A choir may sound excellent in the rehearsal room, but have no idea how they sound after being amplified and projected through the church speakers. Without a sound person to listen and correct the vocal and instrument levels, the choir may sound distorted or too loud or too soft. The careful preparation from rehearsal is for naught if sound quality is lacking during the church service.

This is where a sound person can make all the difference. The sound person can be located towards the rear of the church to hear how the choir sounds to the congregation and then can make any necessary volume and tone adjustments to get the best mix. A sound person can also set up multiple monitors with the choir so that the singers and musicians can hear themselves. A typical sound person in the church is likely a volunteer and not a formally trained music engineer. But if the volunteer understands the mixing board, and is tech-savvy, then they can achieve an excellent sound for the congregation.

If your church is fortunate enough to have a sound person, then before singing and playing, take the time to test your volume level so that you can make an accurate assessment of how you will sound in church. You can ask the sound person to adjust your mix as necessary. For example, if your direct signal from your instrument sounds "clacky," suggest the sound person cut the mid-range, etc., until the desired tone is achieved. If your singing volume is too low or high, ask that it be corrected.

Acoustic Guitar Adjustments

Specific fixes and adjustments can bring out the best tone and action for your guitar. See the "Guitar Player Repair Guide" by Dan Erlewine for a comprehensive review of guitar repair and adjustments. Here is a straightforward upgrade: Whereas many quality acoustic guitars come with plastic bridge pins, many musicians and repairpersons believe that quality bridge pins improve tone. Consider replacing your plastic bridge pins with bone or brass pins, which can be found at most guitar repair shops, or by shopping online. StewMac is a useful website for procuring "luthier" supplies. Note that it is a debated topic regarding whether using quality bridge pins makes a noticeable difference in sound quality. I've had repair professionals tell me that high-end pins make no noticeable difference in tone. Still, I've also read blogs whose writers/players claim that their guitars "came alive" after replacing the pins.

There is another upgrade to consider. If your instrument has low-quality machine heads, or if they're bent and/or broken, you may sound out of tune or hear annoying rattles and buzzes. Install a quality set of machine heads such as Grover tuners on your instrument. Fortunately, machine heads are easily replaceable if you are good with tools and woodworking. But if you're like me and not comfortable repairing your instrument, take your guitar to the repair shop. While your instrument is there, have them inspect the bridge, as well. It should sit flat against the guitar's body with almost no gap between the bridge and the top of the guitar. Not even a thin business card should fit between the bridge and the body. Also, have the repairperson look at the "nut," which sits on your fretboard at the top of your guitar's neck and may need adjustment as well.

Additionally, if your guitar comes with a truss rod in the neck, which many modern acoustic guitars do, then adjustments can be easily made to the neck to improve the action. If your instrument does not have a truss rod, and your action is off, you may need a neck reset, which can be expensive. Check with your repair shop. Making these and other fixes and adjustments to your instrument will supercharge its playability, which will give you that righteous feeling, which in turn translates into better playing. For more information on performing repairs and adjustments, see the "Crimson Custom Guitars" channel on YouTube for helpful instructional videos.

Electric Guitar Adjustments

There are so many subtleties and adjustments necessary to set up and tune an electric guitar that, rather than attempting to discuss that broad topic here, I suggest going to your local, highly recommended guitar repair shop to do it properly, or research do-it-yourself videos.

Wind Instrument Hygiene

If you play a wind instrument, make it a habit to clean out your instrument after every time you play. Disassemble it and swab it down with a quality cleaning product recommended for your instrument to make sure it is clean with all the moisture out. Keeping your wind instrument clean and dry is not only good hygiene, but it also avoids damaging your instrument.

Guard Your Instrument Against the Environment

Wood instruments are especially susceptible to humidity, temperature changes, and moisture in the air. Temperature and humidity changes cause wood to expand and contract, which can crack your instrument and cause other structural damage, which is expensive to fix. Keep your instrument by an inside wall in your home, away from windows, direct sunlight, humidity, in order to avoid wide swings in temperature and moisture that can damage it. Don't leave your instrument by an open window in your house or in the garage where the environment can affect it. In particular, don't leave your instrument out all night in your car, where the ambient environment or rain or snow can damage it. I know a musician who lives in Arizona, who told me that when the summer comes, musicians sometimes forget and leave their instruments in the car for several hours. During the blazing Arizona sun, the inside of a vehicle heats up, and the glue in an instrument's joints warms up and softens. Then the instrument bracings may become loose, and guitars and especially standup basses and cellos can collapse on themselves.

The Big Bang

It doesn't matter how careful I am with my instrument. Over time, it has been dropped, kicked, banged, and/or dinged by me or others. Even when I'm really cautious, I've smacked my guitar into other instruments and had them smack into mine. Accept that your beautiful instrument—the one that you invested in, and play and gently polish, stare at, and take such good care of—will be on the receiving end of bangs, dings, and nicks. Musicians can often recall in vivid detail when and where they were when various injuries befell their instruments. Surprisingly, I've had two different guitar repairmen actually compliment my Martin D-18 and D-35 on their various dings, aging finish, and various battle scars. One repairman even told me that some collectors like dings and scratches because they show the instrument's character and that it has had an active musical life. A long time ago, I thought of having these blemishes sanded and repaired to look like new. But now that I know that battle scars on an instrument are desirable and increase its collectability, I've come to appreciate these blemishes and the tale each one has to tell.

Instrument Cases

According to Dan Erlewine, repairpersons would be out of work if musicians simply put their instruments back in their cases. But on the other hand, an instrument that sits in the case is often un-played. I hang my instruments, including my guitars, violins, and ukes, on my wall using Hercules wall hangers, with the locking clasp. I love to admire the beauty of these instruments, and I like being able to grab one down quickly as the mood strikes me. There is a legitimate question about whether it is harmful to an instrument to hang it on the wall under its own weight, not to mention the chance of it dropping to the ground, especially with earthquakes in California. But I've tried to make my instruments secure and considered the risks, so since I love to have them ready, I'll take my chances. I use a soft case for my instruments when I'm going to play at church and rehearsal because the soft case is lightweight and has lots of storage pockets. I use my hard-shell case when I am playing at unfamiliar venues where the risk of damage is much higher. I always use a hard-shell case for delicate archtops.

Strings, Sound, and Comfort

The type of strings used makes a big difference in how an instrument sounds, how you play it, and how hard your hands have to work. The heavier the gauge string, the more sound an instrument produces, but the harder the string is to press down and the less pliable the string is. If your hands are strong, and you don't have issues with pain, then you can use heavier gauge strings to get the most volume and tone out of your instrument. Lighter strings, including nylon strings for the guitar, can produce a softer, warmer sound, and be much gentler on your fingers, so you won't have to work so hard. But the tradeoff is that you lose volume and that brighter, steel-string tone.

Because many of us use our fingers and wrists constantly, tapping away on computer keyboards and texting on phones, these repetitive movements can injure our hands and wrists. Then, when we play our instrument, our hands and wrists hurt, affecting and limiting our playing. This can be so disheartening. To avoid injuring my hands and wrists, I try to focus on playing more gently, more easily, and relaxed on my instrument. I use different positions and fingerings to avoid repetitive movement and give my fingers different positions to try. Fritz Kreisler, the great violinist, used to run warm water on his fingers before he played, to warm up his hands, and get ready to play.

Also, when I am using my computer, rather than banging hard on the keyboard (which is what I tend to do naturally), I try and type lightly, using proper form and technique, being gentle to my fingers and hands.

By the way, if you have a long document to type, such as an essay or a book, try using the dictation function on your computer. It can really save your hands from strain and injury. I used that function extensively on my Apple computer for this book.

Tuning

Back in high school, my cousin had a band whose friends affectionately dubbed them as "The Tuners." This was because, at parties, the band seemed to forever be tuning their instruments. Today, thanks to electronic tuners, it's so much easier for stringed instruments to be tuned. The more popular tuners clamp to the instrument body, so you can check your tuning while playing. I still keep a pitch pipe in my gig bag as a backup if my tuner batteries die. Also, there are apps that you can download to your device for tuning. If you find yourself continually struggling to keep your instrument in tune, save yourself time and annoyance, and take it to a repair shop for adjustment.

For certain stringed instruments like violins, violas, and standup basses, getting your instrument set up so that it is easy to tune and stays in tune may entail re-boring tuning peg holes so they can more easily be adjusted, installing fine tuners on the tailpiece, and/or making other adjustments to the neck and bridge. My father, Monte, is the most talented musician and singer that I've ever played with, studied classical violin and plays everything from Fritz Kreisler to Kenny Baker. When we play together, he plays his father's old violin, which is over two hundred years old, a magnificent instrument, a testament to that master wood craftsman who made it two centuries ago. And while it's a fantastic-sounding instrument, it has always been temperamental and difficult to tune. When we play, we don't spend a whole lot of time tuning the violin to perfection, which would be too much work and be frustrating. Instead, we get it "pretty close" and then spend our time singing and playing our songs and making music. We recently took this violin to a violin shop in Los Angeles, which came highly recommended. This shop installed a different type of peg on the violin, making precise and accurate tuning easy and quick. It was not an inexpensive repair, but it has really improved the tuning and playing experience. Now when we play together, tuning the violin is super easy.

Figure 5-4 Monte Hill

Tuning a piano is obviously a whole lot different than tuning a violin. Do your research and find a good piano tuner. If your piano needs work, such as sticking pedals or broken keys, you may need to hire a certified piano technician. Local music stores can give you referrals for a qualified piano tuner or technician.

Metronome

Musicians often inadvertently speed up and slow down while playing. Practicing with a metronome can help control your timing and also provide you with a steady beat and a framework to play within. Personally, for nostalgia reasons, I like the old-style wind-up metronome with the mechanical tick. But the digital ones, including the ones available on tablets and cell phones, are more practical and portable. Some sheet music goes the extra mile and even shows you the suggested tempo that the music should be played. You can confirm that tempo using your metronome.

Instrument Cables

Using a cheap cable will inevitably compromise your overall sound. Invest in a quality cable with a good warranty so that if it breaks, you can replace it for free, preferably at the store where you bought it, instead of having to ship it back to the manufacturer. Also, be sure to get the right length that accommodates where you sit or stand at church. The longer the cable, the more chance of you or others tripping on it. Tape down your cables to reduce the tripping hazard. Also, note that some degradation of the signal and/or tone can occur as cable length increases. To avoid loose or noisy connectors, I put a bit of Loctite adhesive on the cable connector threads to prevent the connector from unscrewing. Also, since many cables look alike, mark your cable so that others don't mistake yours for theirs and accidentally walk away with yours. I mark the ends of my cable with red fingernail polish (something my mom taught me) to quickly identify my cable.

Using a wireless system is becoming common and offers the advantages of not having to worry about instrument cables and giving more freedom of movement. But you do have to pay attention to other things, such as keeping your instrument in range of the wireless system, interference from other systems affecting your sound, and ensuring that you maintain batteries in your wireless system.

Instrument Stands

Investing in a quality instrument stand that is stable and easy to carry is a must. When I recently wanted to purchase a stand, I went to my local music store and asked the salesman, who is a musician, which stand he prefers to use. He showed me various models and pointed out that some stands have wider feet, which provides more stability. I ended up choosing an instrument stand with a wider foot stance and with a neck rest to keep my guitar in place.

Don't trust your instrument to a low-quality stand. They can have loose and flimsy joints, and it's hard to pay attention in church when you are worried that your instrument may fall out of its stand. There are many stands to choose from. Do your research and pick one that receives high marks from reviewers and fits your needs.

CHAPTER 6

Listening, Adapting, Contributing

Let the message of Christ dwell among you richly as you
teach and admonish one another with all wisdom through
psalms, hymns, and songs from the Spirit, singing to God
with gratitude in your hearts. —Colossians 3:16

Listening to the Choir and Musicians

When we are singing and playing during church, it is natural for us to focus on our parts. But the problem is, if we focus too much on ourselves, we may ignore the sounds of our fellow vocalists and musicians, and thereby miss an opportunity to blend with the choir and create a more cohesive sound. I recall when I was relatively new to playing with the choir, a choir member mentioned to me that my timing was off. I appreciated the feedback and attempted to adjust my playing so that we sounded more in sync. From that time onward, I decided to really try and listen to those playing beside me— both in rehearsal and in church—and try to blend and adjust my style in real time, as needed. I now really enjoy trying to fit in musically with the vocalists and musicians around me, by playing as a group member and not as an individualist.

Tailoring Your Singing and Playing to the Choir

Listening to and paying close attention to the talents of the other musicians and singers in the choir will change how you sing and play for the better. If we are only listening to our own voice and/or our own instrument, then we won't blend with the mix but instead may begin to sound like a bunch of individuals clashing with each other, rather than like the tight, cohesive choir that we want to be.

Actively listening to your fellow vocalists and musicians will give you ideas about improving and refining your own style. For vocalists, consider if you are singing at the best volume compared with your fellow singers? Are you too loud or too soft? Are you adding vocal dynamics to avoid sounding monotone? Are you thinking about the lyrics as you sing, putting feeling into your voice, and smiling, or are you just singing without thinking? Are you adding vocal vibrato at strategic places? How's your posture? Slouching? Are you singing harmony? If not, can you work with a fellow choir member or take a class to learn to add harmony to your singing?

For musicians, consider if you are playing tightly in sync with the other musicians? Should you alter your tone to make your sound more exciting (but not distracting)? Are you adding lead runs/solos during appropriate spaces in the music? Are you dominating the music in a bad way, overpowering others? Are you playing it too safe, afraid to mess up, and missing opportunities to improvise and be creative? And note that if you do improvise, be intentional and thoughtful. Understand the underlying chord changes, and stay within the scale and tonality of the key.

Patrick O'Brien (introduced in Chapter 2) comments on the importance of blending with other musicians. Patrick says:

> "You need to learn when you are important and when you are not. Understand your role in the piece. Don't just play the notes as written on the page, but understand how you fit into the context of the music and with the other musicians. You should be listening carefully, and you should be aiming to build a cohesive sound with the choir. This skill can take a long time to develop, and many musicians struggle with it."

Recording Your Choir So You Can Improve

As discussed in Chapter 3, recording yourself during rehearsals and church services will refine your skills. When you are singing and playing during the service, you likely won't have time, in the moment, to really listen to the music, because you'll be too busy making it. But if you record the choir, you'll hear yourself and your choir from a more focused and unbiased perspective.

I've found that it can be humbling to hear myself, the way I actually sound, versus how I think I sound. Hearing the playback from the neutral, sometimes cruel honesty of a recorder has put me face-to-face with the limits of my musical skills and shown me where I need to improve. Don't become disheartened if the way you sound coming from the recorder falls short of your expectations. Most artists are their own worst critics. On the other hand, if you are completely satisfied and even impressed with how you sound, you are not critical enough. We can always improve. Another intriguing insight from a recording is to learn we all make mistakes during church service—sometimes big ones—and we think everyone noticed. Yet I've often found that when listening to the playback, there will be a part of a song where I think I really messed up, and I discover that what I thought sounded like a colossal blunder was hardly noticeable at all, except to me.

Creating A Personal, Inspiring Playlist

When you record your choir, you'll be building a unique collection of live, spiritual music that no one else in the world has. The singing, instrumentation, and passion for worship music are unique and different for every choir. Consider that so much of beautiful live music is created every day, every hour, all over the world in churches, coffee shops, schools, and clubs. But since most of this live music is never recorded, it only exists momentarily in listeners' minds and is lost forever. But by recording your choir's music, you can enjoy the lyrics, harmonies, and instruments forever, and enable these musical snapshots to live on, beyond the moment they were created. I have wonderful live recordings from church, practices, Celebrations of Life, family recordings, and live jams while on vacation that I would be very sorry to lose. If you, too, begin to build an audio/video library of recorded live music, ask one of your computer-savvy friends the best way to archive your essential recordings, either to the cloud or to some other external backup hard drive for safekeeping. Otherwise, you may one day irretrievably lose these precious musical memories.

Less is More

Many choirs have multiple musicians playing a variety of instruments. In our choir, we have keyboards, flutes, guitars, a standup bass, a violin, cajón, trombones, and trumpets playing on any given day. Understanding how to play smoothly together with such diverse instruments is challenging. With so many musicians and multiple instruments playing simultaneously, music can begin to sound too busy, like a cluttered garage with random things everywhere. Dan Quigley, the former choir director introduced in Chapter 4, talks about obtaining a good sound with so many musicians:

> "In a small choir, with only a few musicians, there is a lot of room for all the musicians to play a lot. In a large choir with multiple musicians, the best approach is for the musicians to simplify their playing and play less. If I, as the keyboard player, am surrounded by three guitar players, I often will choose to play just a simple triad chord, say a C major, only using three notes. I may use my left hand only, no pedals, and leave more space for the other musicians to play. Interestingly, many musicians find it difficult to play less, and to leave openings and holes to avoid over-crowding the music."

A choir composed of many musicians should therefore consider keeping instrumentation light and minimal. For example, when multiple guitarists are playing, they should try and decrease their individual playing to leave more space and holes in the music. In his excellent video entitled "The Guitar of Brian Setzer," Brian Setzer makes the point that a guitarist often best accompanies a vocalist by playing only three or four strings in a chord, and not six. An abbreviated chord allows the singers to dominate.

In a musically crowded choir, instruments like violins and wind instruments may choose to simplify their playing and focus more on playing harmony, or descant at strategic points in the song, or add connecting runs and flourishes here and there, rather than playing the whole time or duplicating the melody being sung by the choir. Henry

Poblete, the flutist introduced in Chapter 4, offers his attitude on playing with a large choir:

> "I don't worry about how many musicians there are, or which instruments they are playing. As long as the musicians are good, I enjoy playing with a larger band. I just adjust my playing to fit the situation, and don't worry about it."

Silence is Golden

Whereas the guiding principle for a doctor is "Physician, do no harm," similarly, there will be times when you as a singer or musician are supposed to sing or play a particular song for church, but you decide to just sit this one out. Maybe the song is not in your vocal range, the timing is tricky, or you really don't like it. Whatever the reason, if you're just not feeling it, you may choose to adopt the physician's principle and "do no harm." To do this, simply minimize your contribution. If you're one of several vocalists, just sing silently. If you are one of multiple musicians, just turn down your volume and play silently. Go into listening mode, and enjoy listening to your choir. Especially if you are in a medium to larger choir, you don't need to tell the choir that you are sitting this one out; they will most likely be focused on themselves. Obviously, if you are supposed to sing solo, then you must do that to the best of your ability, whether or not you are excited about the piece. But knowing when not to sing and when not to play, may, in certain situations, be your best contribution. Apply the old axiom, "Only speak, when speaking improves on silence."

Developing Your Own Style

Contributing something vocally or musically memorable in a choir can be challenging, especially when you are surrounded by talented vocalists and musicians. With so many talented singers and musicians all around you, how can you develop your own style and make a unique musical contribution?

George Harrison's musical evolution provides us with some inspiration on how to grow as an artist. Back in the early days of the Beatles, John Lennon and Paul McCartney would write a song and then ask Harrison to create a guitar solo for it. Harrison's solo would need to fit within a short number of measures, be completed under a tight schedule, and be acceptable to Lennon and McCartney. Harrison at that time had not fully developed his talents. Since the Lennon/McCartney songwriting team was so prolific, Harrison was only allowed to record one of his original songs per album; he felt marginalized. Although obscured in the shadow of Lennon and McCartney, Harrison worked hard to improve as a musician and songwriter, and he did improve. In fact, he became so good that today when Beatles fans are polled to pick their favorite Beatles songs, Harrison's compositions, such as "Something," "While My Guitar Gently Weeps," and "Here Comes the Sun," are often preferred by fans over Lennon/McCartney compositions.

How could Harrison improve so much as a musician and a songwriter and develop his own unique style to such a high degree of achievement? The answer: talent, hard work, and, most importantly, he believed in himself and did not allow others to define or put him in a box. Let us likewise not be disheartened or discouraged if others try to put us down or limit our potential—let us work hard and strive to be the best singers and musicians that we can be, and grow on our journey.

As vocalists and musicians, we may aspire to sing and play in a style way that is unique to us, which reflects our own strengths and talents. Brian Setzer is an excellent example of a musician who chooses to not play in a dull or monotonous manner. Setzer is known for meshing different styles together—and playing in an exciting, refreshing way. In a single song, he may play with a flat pick, change to fingerpicking, and change again to brushing chords using his thumb. For Setzer, the fun of music is to blend different musical styles together, such as rock, jazz, classical, and country, to give the listener something unique and unexpected to listen to. Listen, for example, to Setzer's "Stray Cat Strut."

To develop your own style, try adapting Setzer's philosophy; reach into your musical toolbox and pull out all the styles that you love best, be they classical, jazz, Spanish, R&B, reggae, rock, country—whatever you love. Then when you sing or play, add your favorites styles into the song so that your sound is exciting and unique and not a boring, redundant monotony of notes played in the same way, with the same tempo and dynamics. As you play the styles that you love, your musical choices will cause your own unique style to emerge.

Fritz Kreisler, one of the greatest violinists who ever lived, was loved in his time and celebrated worldwide for his passionate style of playing and his focus on obtaining a beautiful, emotion-filled tone. Kreisler had a unique perspective on how to play with individual style. He believed that music, at its core, is an expression of the character, personality, and inner qualities of the musician. Becoming a great musician, Kreisler believed, was not about technical proficiency, but about projecting the musician's inner feelings, character, and emotions into the music. Music, Kreisler, thought, is a manifestation of the person who is playing. Thus, for a person to sing or play in a manner that moves and connects with her audience, that singer or musician must genuinely feel joy, fear, anger, and gladness as they sing and play so that those feelings are felt by the audience. Kreisler said, "When I play, I am completely myself, and I have no fear of being misunderstood." If we as vocalists and musicians can sing and play music with honesty, authenticity, and be ourselves, perhaps we too can connect with the congregation in a style that reflects who we really are.

Play Melody

Playing solos is an area that I continue to work on, but it is not one of my strengths. But I think you will agree that hearing a beautiful melody played by a good musician is one of life's great pleasures. Question: If you are a musician and you are asked to take a solo break, and you have the discretion to improvise your own solo, what notes should you play? There are so many options to choose from. You could create a cool jazz, rock, or classically inspired solo break that fits with the piece, but is also surprising and creative. But before deciding to improvise a new solo for the piece, consider that perhaps you should just play the melody. At first blush, you may think that playing the melody as your solo is boring and predictable, but bear in mind that the congregation really loves to hear the melody to songs that they know, especially if the melody is played really well and is catchy. I think in church, especially, where there are so many beautiful melodies and memorable phrases in Christian music, playing the melody is a solid choice for a solo.

Integrating Your Playing With the Keyboard

In many choirs, the keyboard is the rock upon which the choir is built. If there were no other choir instruments, the choir would still sound good with only keyboard accompaniment. This is because the keyboard is such a multidimensional, multifaceted instrument. Its genius is that, like the guitar, it is one of the few instruments that can combine melody, bass, rhythm, percussion, and pedal effects in one instrument, all at the same time.

It's a worthy exercise for musicians to record and listen to how they sound playing with the keyboard. Depending on the instrument that you play, you may be surprised to hear that, at times, you may sound out of sync with the keyboard. This may be because the keyboard is playing a different rhythm pattern or tempo than you are, and it may feel awkward for you to get in sync. From a mechanical point of view, rhythmic divergences among different instruments are understandable, given the different ways that musicians make sounds on their instruments. A pianist strikes keys with downward hand and finger strokes, moves from side-to-side, pauses in the air, and uses foot pedals and dynamics to achieve tonal effects. On the other hand, musicians on other stringed instruments, such as violins, cellos, bass, and guitars, strike the strings in very different ways from the pianist, with their hands and fingers pressing down on strings and sliding up and down the neck, using vibrato, right or left hands using bows, picks, and fingers to attack strings. Woodwind instruments create music using breath and unique finger movements, pressing on keys—again very different from the keyboard.

The art of blending well with the keyboard should be a priority for choir musicians. In many church choirs, the keyboard is the main instrument. So, adjust your playing to complement the keyboard and not clash with it. If the keyboard player is active and plays many chords and melody lines, consider playing your instrument less, but more strategically. Think about how best to integrate your playing with the keyboard and with other musicians. This stylistic calculation varies from pianist to pianist, and from organist to organist, as each individual player has their own style. I think you will enjoy, as I have, the challenge of trying to integrate your sound with the keyboard and trying to find a complementary style with different pianists.

Fingerpicking Guitar with the Keyboard

Certain worship songs, especially the more beautiful ones, sound exceptionally good when fingerpicked on the guitar. It's worth investing in lessons with a classical guitar teacher to learn the basic patterns and techniques for fingerstyle guitar. And one of the more beautiful sounds in music is when a piano player and a string player (such as guitar, violin, viola, or cello) play closely together, where the musicians know each other well and have played together a long time. For example, listen to the fantastic collaboration between Carole King and James Taylor on their video "Live at the Troubadour" and how Taylor's superb fingerpicking complements King's piano. There is a lost generation of master fingerstyle guitarists, who have either passed away or have become overlooked, and are fading from memory. These fingerstyle players focused on an expressive and aggressive fingerpicking style, using unique chord shapes, walking bass lines, and highly developed fingerpicking techniques. Thank goodness videos of these masters survive, and we can see for ourselves the complexity of their guitar work. Table 6-1 below lists some of my favorite fingerstyle guitar players and references to some of my favorite examples.

Table 6-1 Fingerstyle Guitar Masters

ARTIST	SONG	NOTES
Merle Travis	"I'll See You in My Dreams" and "Farewell My Bluebell"	Melody, bass, and accompaniment played by Travis, all at the same time. Note the rhythmic, percussive thumb sound.
Chet Atkins	"Baby's Coming Home," and "Happy Again"	Master of precise tone, technique, and timing.
Jerry Reed and Chet Atkins	"Jerry's Breakdown" (see video)	Two friends and fingerpickers, both at the top of their game.
Jim Croce and Maury Muehleisen	"Operator"	Croce sometimes uses fingerpicks on three fingers, in addition to a thumb pick—a technique rarely seen today. Marvel at the talent of Jim's lead guitarist, Maury Muehleisen. Both died in the same plane crash.
James Taylor	"Sweet Baby James"	Powerful use of descending bass notes and unique hammer-ons.
Brian Setzer	"Sleep Walk" (video, live at the Ryman). Also, listen to "You Can't Hurry Love"	Hybrid flat pick and fingerpicking with a mix of jazz and rockabilly styles.
Scotty Moore (with Elvis Presley)	"Blue Moon of Kentucky" and "Just Because"	Sun Session recordings. Note the thumbpicking in a rockabilly style. Carl Perkins is also preeminent in this style.

In addition to the guitarists listed in the above table, other notable guitarists include the great Andrés Segovia, who created a whole different genre and style for classical guitar, as well as other contemporary fingerstyle electric guitar players, such as Mark Knopfler (Dire Straits), Lindsey Buckingham (Fleetwood Mac), and dazzling country players such as Glen Campbell and Roy Clark.

Using a Flat Pick on Guitar

As expressive as fingerpicking is, the steady rhythm of a flat pick on a guitar provides a strong accompaniment that helps keep the choir in time. Considerations such as choosing the right gauge pick, which strings to strike, and where to position the pick—closer to the soundhole, bridge, or neck—give unlimited opportunities to change the feel, tone, and impact of the guitar.

Rumbling the Bass Strings

Depending on the instrument that you play, emphasizing the lower bass registers instead of mostly playing the higher notes can provide a fuller sound. I notice the great bluegrass fiddle player Alison Krauss often plays melodies and runs in the lower registers, making for a smoother, mellower sound compared to the thinness that higher strings on the violin sometimes produce. Depending on the instrument being played, it's easy for musicians to default to playing in the higher treble registers and forget to emphasize the bass notes. If your choir does not have a standup or electric bass and primarily produces treble sounds, the choir's overall tone can come across as shrill, lacking depth and bottom. Guitarists often use capos (see discussion below), which can exacerbate this problem by further raising the pitch of the music. If your choir sounds too trebly or shrill, and without enough bottom end, try focusing your playing on the lower strings to add a lower contrast.

Guitar Thumb Picking

The thumb pick enables the low bass notes to ring with power. Having a thumb pick that's too bulky, thick, or cumbersome can make you play too heavy on the strings. But having too thin of a thumb pick can make it feel like you can't apply enough power, or the thumb pick is going to slip off. Experiment to find the right thumb pick for you. For an advanced fingerpicking style that does not use a thumb pick, check out the style of Brian Setzer. He holds a flat pick in the typical fashion. But, when he wants to fingerpick, Setzer tucks his pick into his index finger and fingerpicks with just his fingers and thumb. While this is a challenging style to master, it affords you many attractive stylistic opportunities. See "The Guitar of Brian Seltzer" to explore this style. Instead of using Setzer's method, some guitarists just put the pick between their index and middle fingers while fingerpicking. Others put the pick in their mouth while they fingerpick which also works well but is less elegant, not to mention less hygienic.

Palm Muting on Guitar

I love the percussive sound of muted strings. The idea is that, rather than always letting the bass strings ring out bright and sustained, you can use the palm of your picking hand to mute the lower bass strings on your instrument, which on the guitar would be the E, A, D strings for a percussive effect. By palm muting bass strings, you give variety and power to your sound. On the guitar, try muting the bass strings with your palm while at the same, picking the higher strings (G, B, E on guitar) as usual. You'll find that the combination of muted bass strings with ringing, sustained treble strings is a pleasing sound to the ear. For an exceptional example video of this picking style, see Thom Bresh's, "The Guitar of Merle Travis."

Altering Hand Position on Guitar

For the guitarist, a simple technique that Merle Travis and Chet Atkins employed to naturally change their guitar tone (without using any pedals) was to move their picking hand away from its standard playing position (which is around the middle of the guitar) down to a position around by the twelfth fret. Picking with your right hand at around the twelfth fret instead of being above the soundhole is an easy, low-tech way to change your instrument's tone. The same applies to the viola, violin, cello, standup bass, etc. If you place the bow either more towards the neck or more towards the bridge, a different sound is produced, giving you more tonal options.

When it comes to playing the guitar and hand position, it's been said, "There's no money above the fifth fret." But since many church musicians often don't get paid anyway, it's fun to get out of your conform zone, and play higher up the neck. Many new, exciting positions, chord shapes, double-stops, fingerings, and rhythms await musicians who venture high up the neck. To see an example of a virtuoso guitarist creating unique chord shapes higher up on the neck, rather than using boring chords in the first position, watch Peter Frampton play "Baby, I Love Your Way."

The Capo

The capo is another super-convenient tool for a church guitarist. Since worship music is often not written in guitar-friendly keys, playing descending bass lines, hammer-ons, open chords, and other conventional guitar techniques becomes more difficult without a capo. The capo helps alleviate this issue because it enables guitarists to use easier chord shapes while playing in different key signatures. Tip: If you use a capo, make sure and double-check your tuning after installing the capo, because once it is in place, the pressure and position of the capo, may change your intonation.

Further, using the capo is an excellent way to produce more diverse tones among multiple instruments. For example, two guitarists playing without a capo can sound monotonous because they are in the same tonal register. But if one of the guitarists uses a capo, this creates a nice variation in tone and can make the overall sound more interesting. But understanding where to place the capo, what key you were in with a capo versus without, and how to be in the correct key with other guitarists and instruments, like the piano, can be confusing. For more information, go to the Shubb capo website for explanations on how to use the capo.

Although a capo is an essential tool for your gig bag, and I love the ease of transposition that it affords, I mostly prefer to play without one. Personally, I think my guitar sounds fuller without using a capo, and I don't like putting what feels like a clamp on the neck of my guitar. I also like the musical challenge of playing the actual, albeit more difficult, chord shapes that the keyboardist is playing. If you choose to minimize your use of the capo, the benefit is that you'll play less common chords, lots of bar chords higher up the neck, and interesting chord shapes that you might not have otherwise played.

CHAPTER 7

The Children's/Youth Choir

And his gifts were that some should be apostles, some prophets,
some evangelists, some pastors and teachers... —Ephesians 4:11-13

There are so many wonderful reasons to form a children's/youth choir, the most significant being to instill in children a belief in God. Rather than learning about faith only through Sunday school, children who join the choir can learn about faith by singing songs in a spiritual setting. I've talked to so many adults who trace the beginnings of their faith to childhood experiences in the church choir.

In addition to sowing seeds of faith in a child, there are other substantial benefits for children who participate in a church choir. These include developing self-esteem, confidence, and a sense of teamwork. Children who join the choir may also discover a hidden musical talent that they never knew they had. Learning to sing and play an instrument, especially at a young age, can become a lifelong love, companion, and remedy to boredom and stress.

If the choir performs or attends concerts, plays, and musicals, these experiences further help a child develop an appreciation of music and the arts. When I was about nine years old, my cousin, David, who was and still is, a great man of faith, took me to a production of the musical "Camelot." The actors were young and dressed in colorful exotic costumes. The musical was performed in a small theater, perhaps it was a church or high school theater, and it was packed. David and I just leaned against the wall in the rear of the venue, and watched the performance. At first, I was a bit bored, never having watched a play before and not understanding the plot or dialogue. But gradually, I began to enjoy the play, the singing, the excitement of live performance. And I was attracted to that famous repeating refrain, which I still remember and was a favorite of President Kennedy:

> "Don't let it be forgot
> That once there was a spot
> For one brief shining moment
> that was known as Camelot"

By introducing children to faith, music, and the arts at a young age, we can truly make a lasting positive impression on their lives.

Social Benefits of Choir for Children

Children will not only grow spiritually in the choir, but socially as well. The choir can expand a child's social network by introducing a whole new set of friends, different from the ones they know at school and around the neighborhood.

Joe Demurs, who served in the U.S. Army for twenty two years and played French horn in the army band, offers an insight. When Joe retired as a Sergeant First Class from the Army, he was hired as a choir director at Eastlake High School in Chula Vista, and he now plays piano at various local venues and clubs around San Diego. Joe says that he saw many students begin in the choir, very shy and afraid to sing in front of a group. But after joining the choir, a transformation often occurs; children start to love to sing and play so much that as Joe said, "you almost have to tear the microphone out of their hand to get them off the stage."

Alicia McMillan, who is the Director of Worship and Music at Point Loma Community Presbyterian Church in Point Loma, California, is a brilliant and innovative educator and has worked with children for the past twenty years. She loves the choir and draws upon her wealth of knowledge and insight to nurture and grow the children in faith and music. Each year at Christmastime, Alicia prepares and directs the children's and youth choirs in a splendid production of Christmas music, helping to spread the joy and hope of Christmas. The children's and youth choirs perform together accompanied by musicians from the San Diego Symphony, with Alicia directing the choir and also accompanying on a magnificent organ. Alicia points out:

> "One of the biggest blessings working with children is to be able to witness their progress and growth from season to season. I have seen so many children who start out insecure and shy and after a few seasons in the choir, sing solos and perform acting roles. We encourage them season-by-season and give them bigger parts, and they step up and blossom. One parent of a four-year-old thanked me for teaching her child to pronounce words—the parent said that her child's reading skills improved as a result of the choir."

Figure 7-1 Alicia McMillan

As discussed in Chapter 4, the church choir is not about "performance." Still, children will develop confidence and stage presence as a result of being in the choir. This self-assuredness benefits them greatly as they go through school and begin working. And let's not forget how wonderful the teacher/choir director feels when they witness children who struggled to sing or were shy find confidence and strength and blossom through the choir.

Emilie Erickson is sixteen years old and belongs to the Good Shepherd Church, whose choir contains a mix of teenagers and young adults. Emilie says she has truly enjoyed her choir experience and discovered that she loves to sing. Now that Emilie is part of the choir, her whole family makes it a point to go to church each Sunday to hear her sing, which is a magnificent thing. Emilie says about how she first joined the choir:

"I used to feel like I was being dragged to church. I dreaded it, just sitting there, being quiet until the end. Then I saw a church bulletin that said: "Join the Choir." So, I joined, and something snapped. Now, I don't dread going to church. Now, I can express myself. I have made amazing new friends, have an awesome choir director, and I just don't have to sit there being quiet. Choir, church, and music can impact your life, just as it has mine."

More from Emilie on her choir experience:

"I've found that singing takes away any stress that I have in my day. We practice the music to the songs in our hymnals, and if we get out of tune, are singing too quietly, or making mistakes, we stop and fix our part. I go to rehearsal once each week, and we do the songs over and over. Right before we practice, we say the Lord's Prayer."

Figure 7-2 Emilie Erickson

Auditions for Children/Youth Choir?

A discussion about auditions for the adult choir is provided in Chapter 3. But should there be auditions to join the children's/youth choir? Based on my interviews with those in the field, the consensus is no. The central purpose of the choir is to teach children about faith through music, not to become famous or sign a record deal. The choir directors that I have spoken with believe that any child who wants to join should be welcomed to do so. We are striving to mentor, teach, and inspire the next generation of believers, so denying entry to the choir because of any mere musical limitation, and potentially injuring a young, fragile spirit, would be a misplaced priority. Additionally, from a vocal perspective, many authorities believe that singing is a learned behavior and that all children can learn how to sing.

There are exceptions where auditions would be appropriate. For example, if your church is putting on a musical play or special event, where someone needs to play a lead role, with other children having supporting roles, auditions are beneficial to see where to place a child and what role they are best suited to play. In fact, the audition process itself can become a good learning experience for the choir, as children learn to study and perform their part and work together as a team. If you do hold auditions, it is vital to ensure that all children participate in the auditions and that each child has a special part, even if it's a small one in the production, so that all the children share in the fun.

Organizing Children's/Youth Choir by Age Groups

If your church is lucky to have a large choir with children of various ages, then consider dividing the children and youth into groups according to grade levels so that the children fit and work together well. Separating children by grade levels helps provide an effective mix of choir students because it aligns them with other children at their relative developmental level. There are lots of combinations depending on the age mix of your choir. Here are potential choir grouping discussed by Helen Kemp, in her classic work on children's choir, entitled "Of Primary Importance," by grade level:

- Group 1: Pre-school through first grade (children's choir) (taught by rote)
- Group 2: Second through fifth grade or second through sixth grade (children's choir) (taught with music)
- Group 3: Sixth or seventh grade through twelfth grade (youth choir)

But if your children's choir is like many and only has a small number of children, and if you have trouble maintaining sufficient members in your choir, you will need to mix the various ages together as best you can. And sometimes, siblings, who may span different ages, want to sing together, and allowing them to be together can be more convenient for their parents.

Nuances of Young Voices

Generally speaking, children in pre-school through the first grade do not have the physical ability, either in lung capacity or vocal maturity, to project their voices loudly and produce a consistently pleasing tone. When very young children attempt to project their voices powerfully, their tone can resemble something more like a scream. Vocal cords, lungs, abdomen, and diaphragm need years to fully develop. By the second grade, however, there is often a marked improvement in the overall tone and breath support of a child's singing voice. Also, by the second grade, children are becoming better readers, which means they can read the lyrics to the songs.

During middle school, you may notice that girls' voices tend to become weaker and airier, and boys' voices begin to change as well. A choir director needs to be careful to not push children's voices too hard during these times. At the same time, children need to continue singing during these vocally challenging years to continue to build their vocal skills. After puberty, children's voices will change and become much stronger.

Accessing Children's Vocal Skills and Doing Assessments

It's beneficial to evaluate a child's musical strengths and areas for improvement. As you assess the voices in your choir, you will gain a better understanding of the overall skill level in your group, and you can offer vocal exercises and techniques to help the choir improve.

One way to do an assessment is to schedule a private, one-on-one session with a child to gauge their musical strengths and weaknesses. In Helen Kemp's book, "Of Primary Importance," she suggests having a one-on-one meeting with each child and asking them to sing an easy song like "Happy Birthday" or "Jingle Bells" to evaluate their skills. Can they match pitch, or can they sing on pitch? Does their voice wander off-key? Can they sing equally well in their chest voice and their head voice? See more on the chest and head voice below. Is their tone nasal, light, pushed, airy, etc.? Kemp suggests keeping a written log for each child to characterize vocal strengths and note areas for improvement.

Alternately, you may choose to meet with a group of four or five children at the same time and have them sing to you as a group. This group approach may be more comfortable for you and less intimidating to the child.

Whichever way the assessment is done, find a low-key, non-scary way to evaluate each child's talents and skills. Then, work with them to develop their skills in fun and creative ways.

Choose Music Arranged in the Correct Vocal Range for Young Voices

Because children's voices are still developing, a choir director must select music written in the proper range for children's voices to sing comfortably. Children should be encouraged to sing in their middle range, which should feel most comfortable, given their limited vocal capabilities. Unfortunately, so much of published children's church music is in the wrong vocal range for them, as it's often pitched too low for their voices. Young children have trouble hitting middle C and low A. And some choir directors, who don't know any better, buy the wrong music, written in the wrong range. Be selective about the music that you choose, and make sure it is written in the proper range. The Choristers Guild, an organization that focuses on supporting children's choir, publishes music for children's choir in the appropriate ranges. Go to https://www.choristersguild.org for information and resources.

Choose Music that Children Love to Sing

Besides choosing music that is pitched correctly, select music that the children/youth will love to sing, and that has a great spiritual message. Young people don't want to sing music that is boring and without a meaningful message. Do your research, go to YouTube, the Choristers Guild website, listen to other children's choirs, review music books, and choose engaging, meaningful music for your choir. Also, take time to explain the meaning of the lyrics, what is special about a song, and how does it offer hope, comfort, or inspiration to the congregation. And if the words to the song originated from the Bible, read the actual verse so children see the connection between the song and the Bible. This is an excellent opportunity to teach children new vocabulary or Biblical stories and concepts.

Sing in "Head Voice," Not "Chest Voice"

Alicia is convinced that singing on pitch is a learned behavior and can be taught to all children over time. She believes it is crucial to develop a child's "head voice" and the ability to sing high pitches at an early age rather than singing predominantly in lower pitches in their "chest voice." The chest voice can generally be defined as someone's natural talking voice, which uses the voice's lower registers. When singing in your chest voice, if you place your hand on your upper chest, you will feel a vibration. When singing in your head voice in the higher registers, you won't feel that same vibration. Regarding the connection between singing and pitch issues, Alicia says:

"It is important to teach children to sing in their head voice and develop their high range. The beautiful light tone of children's voices is found primarily in the head voice. Some children with no singing experience sing exclusively in their chest voice and have difficulty or are unable to sing high. Most of these children also have difficulty with pitch matching and tend to sing monotone or very low. Children need to learn what it feels like to sing high and learn to listen and match pitch. Many are unaware that they are not matching pitch or not singing in unison with the group."

Alicia uses innovative and fun exercises to help children hear and feel their head voice. Her choir works on activities at each rehearsal to improve their skills. Alicia says:

"The best way I found to teach children to sing in their head voice is through the use of fun games and vocalizations. Creating sound effects of sirens, throwing stuffed animals up progressively higher (flying dog game), 'Mickey Mouse' voice, imitating animal sounds such as owls, cats, whining like a horse or a puppy, coyote, donkey (both head and chest voice), cow, baby birds, squeaking doors, etc. all get done in their head voice. All ages love these fun vocal explorations."

Pitch Issues

For some children, singing comes naturally, and staying in pitch is relatively easy. But for others, singing in pitch takes more practice. Some children will have trouble matching their voice to the notes played on the piano or to notes sung by their fellow choir members. Their voices tend to wander off-key or go flat or sharp, and they lose the melody. Often times, these children won't even be aware that they are singing flat or sharp and out of key. Alicia makes the point:

"Young children also have to learn to distinguish high from low sounds; many can't tell the difference at a young age. If a child is really struggling with pitch matching, the best method I found is to get close to that child and ask them to slide up or down to the pitch you are singing. If that doesn't work, try matching the pitch the child is singing first and then have them experiment by sliding up/down to find your pitch. This will enable the child to listen and to get direct feedback on pitch matching. I've taught many children who could not match pitch or find their head voice. Over time they all learned how to do it and developed beautiful singing voices. Many ended up singing solos in our church musicals using both their head and chest voices successfully. It is always such a joy to watch this transformation!"

Children's Choir Rehearsal

Arlene Belenzo, who volunteers as a choir director for Mater Dei Catholic Church in Chula Vista, focuses primarily on directing the children and youth choir. When Arlene was thirteen, she saw an invitation to join the teen choir in the church bulletin, answered the call, and has been active in various church choirs ever since. Arlene is one of those individuals who has a natural intuition for teaching children, a gift for teaching that is hard to describe but easy to recognize. She leads the choir, smiling, making little jokes, encouraging the choir, giving direction, asking now and then for an "Amen!" to confirm the children are listening. The mood is light and fun, but there is also a sense of mission and purpose. Arlene is quick to ask for quiet from the children and redirect any child back on task, which gently reminds the children and parents that we are there to serve. Arlene says a prayer at the beginning and end of choir practice, one which seems to have been created in real-time, on the spot, inspiring for this day. On the subject of helping children with pitch issues, Arlene says:

"There are children who especially need to learn the skill of listening carefully to other children singing and the notes being played on the piano so that they learn to match the notes. By coming every week to practice, singing in church, and practicing on their own and at home, I definitely hear them improve. If a child is having trouble singing on pitch, then as they begin in choir, I may ask them to sing a little softer and listen carefully to their neighbor until they become more confident. We also work on using their whole vocal instrument, including their mouth, diaphragm, core, and posture. I work with them one-on-one if needed, but usually, we work on pitch together as a group."

For children and youth who step up to the podium to cantor during church service, Arlene makes sure that they practice their solo well in advance. She provides the children with a digital recording of their rehearsal either on their cell phone or e-mails it to their parents. She asks her students to practice at least three times a day and listen to the recording of themselves while brushing their teeth, riding in the car, or whenever.

Do Children Need to Read Music for Choir?

It is challenging to teach young children to read music because doing it is a step-by-step process that builds upon itself over the years. And because there is usually so much turnover in children's choir, there is often not enough time and continuity to teach it. But teaching children the basics of reading music is a worthy goal. Joe Demurs, who has taught fourteen- to eighteen-year-old students in choir, piano, and guitar class to read music at Eastlake High School in Chula Vista, says:

"Students were reluctant to try to learn to read music at first, but I always emphasized that music is just another language that you can become fluent in. It builds on itself, using basic math and graphics principles. As the students saw others around them

117

picking it up, they realized it was achievable, and started to have fun and success. Whether the student was a singer or musician, I used the piano to teach, because the keyboard lays music principles out visually. The end goal was that after a couple years in class, the student could plunk out a simple melody and chords, and play scales."

If you are teaching children about reading music, research the "solfège" system, which uses hand signals to teach basic music reading skills and rhythm syllables for understanding rhythms.

Motivating Children to Stay in Choir

There are unique considerations for working with children versus working with an adult choir. For one thing, you usually won't know what kind of day a child has had before coming to the choir. Perhaps they had a rough day at school, are not feeling well, or are facing family stresses that affect their behavior and mood.

Such external factors can impact how a child feels and may cause the child—who lacks adult maturity—to misbehave or be distracted during choir. It's crucial to remind yourself that each child is an individual with unique motivations, behaviors, and needs. Our goal is to help the children learn about faith and have fun singing together. As teachers, we need to have an abundance of understanding, compassion, and patience for this next generation of believers.

Plan to have fun and exciting things for the kids to do, so that they look forward to coming to choir, seeing their friends, and singing. Let the children know that by singing in church, they can change another person's mood for the better. There may be an anxious or depressed person sitting in the pews, and the choir can make that person smile and give them hope and inspiration. Let the children know that by serving in the choir, they are serving God.

> *Before I formed you in the womb I knew you,*
> *and before you were born I consecrated you,*
> *I appointed you a prophet to the nations.* —Jeremiah 1:5

While learning to sing well is a worthy goal, the point of the church choir is not about becoming musical superstars, but about helping children grow in their faith. If the choir environment is too strict, too severe, and no fun, the children will feel like the choir is forced on them, and they'll drop out.

Shayne McIntyre, is a former educator at the Christian-based Rock Church in Point Loma, and has traveled all over the world, producing his own TV series, "On Surfari." Shayne can currently be seen on "Beyond Waves". He brings his love of adventure, enthusiasm, and an always-present, teachable faith to young people. Shayne says regarding motivating children:

"I've found that one of the most important things for motivating children is that children want to know that you care about them. It's huge for them to know that you really care. I tell my students that I value them. I get to know them, and I learn about their interests. Jesus was a teacher, and Jesus always let people know that he cared for and loved them. Later on, if you have to discipline a child in some way or correct their behavior, then they will know that you care about them, and that really helps."

Try and understand what motivates children to come to the choir, and set them up for success. Find out what their personal interests are and incorporate those into choir practices. Encourage the children to share their ideas for things that they want to do during practices, to make it fun and something to look forward to. For those who are new to teaching, Shayne recommends a book by Harry and Rosemary Wong, entitled "The First Days of School: How to Be An Effective Teacher" as an excellent primer.

Figure 7-3 Shayne McIntyre

Arlene Belenzo says it is vital to teach the children that we are there to serve (not "perform"), to learn our faith, and have fun in the choir. Arlene makes the point that there are challenges in retaining children/youth in the choir:

"It does take a time investment by the children and parents to prepare and serve in the choir. There is a lot to learn at first, almost like learning a new language. A huge challenge is that children are so busy! Many children and youth are involved in sports and other activities, and attending choir often loses out to sports and their other commitments. As children grow older and join the youth choir, attendance problems become worse because young adults are now juggling their own priorities, and again, attending choir becomes last on their list."

One way to attract children to the choir and gain the support and involvement of the parents is to put on a musical production a couple of times each year, where the children get an opportunity to act, sing, and play instruments. Children and parents love participating in musical plays and productions. Although these productions require a gargantuan amount of work in preparation, rehearsal, and performance, this can also be a great way to recruit children for the choir.

Children's Choir Events and Extracurricular Activities

Look for opportunities to involve the children's choir in extracurricular church activities and events to share their gifts and inspire others in your church. A few examples below:

1. Feature the children's choir in various morning, noon, and evening church services throughout the year. The congregation will be inspired by the choir.
2. Speak with the Sunday school teachers, youth ministry, healing ministry, fundraising ministry, etc., to see if there are

any opportunities for the children's choir to sing or help out with special projects.

3. Mother's and Father's Day are the perfect days to have the children's choir participate in a special tribute to mothers and fathers.

4. Bazaars, raffles, outdoor church festivals, and fundraisers are great events for the children/youth choir to sing at.

5. Organize a "Bless Your Pet Day" (described in Chapter 8). This is a fantastic event for the children's choir to sing at, as children love pets.

6. Christmas and Easter are special times when the children's choir can really shine by singing in plays and musicals, which may also include dancing. These events do take tremendous work and rehearsal, but they also help with recruiting new members to the choir.

7. Combine the adult and children's choirs and sing together across the generations.

Naturally, doing these extracurricular activities takes a lot of work, organization, and rehearsal. Still, the rewards are great as the children grow and flourish in their faith, music, and fellowship.

Managing and Teaching Your Choir Class

You won't be able to teach children about faith, music, or anything if you can't control your choir class. But how do you manage and motivate a roomful of children, especially if you are not a trained educator? Teaching a children's choir class can be difficult if you are with children who have challenges at home, who may be experiencing family break-ups, have behavioral issues, or whose families are struggling financially.

Yet such children are the very ones who can benefit most from being in the choir and the example you set as a teacher/choir director. If you notice that a child seems to be having an issue, be it a sudden lack of attendance or some other problem, set up time to talk with the parents so that you can better understand what the issue is.

Make sure that you set realistic expectations for yourself regarding the children. Remind yourself that the children and youth in the choir are immature, that they will misbehave, not pay attention, talk out of turn, etc. Understand and accept that the children will make many mistakes. Show them compassion, patience, and understanding as you teach. As a faith-based teacher, you are a huge example to them, so strive to be an excellent one.

If possible, consider having a junior volunteer help you manage the class. Having a young volunteer will be a great help to you, and the children will benefit from having an additional assistant, who they can look up to. Also, volunteers may be able to earn credit at their school for helping out in the classroom. It is beneficial to have a simple poster with a few positively stated rules such as:

- Be Kind and Respectful
- Listen, Keep Your Hands to Yourselves
- Follow Directions

Talk at the beginning of the choir season about these rules and why they are important, such as the rules help to keep us safe. Consider having a policy such as "three strikes and you're out" where children get three warnings for not following rules, and on the third one, they have to sit out. When they are ready to follow the rules, they can rejoin the group. Inform the parent if a child had to sit out or had significant behavioral issues.

Cherish the children and the choir. Choir time is your opportunity to reach the children, teach them, and inspire them in faith and music. It doesn't really matter if a child sings well or not, but you, through your teaching style, can be a guiding light to that child and change their life for the better. Table 7-1 provides suggestions for helping children to enjoy their choir time and keep them wanting to come back.

Table 7-1 Tips for Teaching and Managing Children's Choir

TIPS	EXPLANATION
Prayer	At the beginning of choir practice, say a prayer, and/or ask the children to lead in prayer. This puts everyone in a good spiritual frame of mind. Consider saying a prayer at the end of practice as well.
Keep it fun, and if you feed them, they will come	Keep choir practice fun, enjoyable, and productive. Children love food, so feed them snacks (but be aware and very careful of any food sensitivities any children may have). Find fun games to play and give small rewards as prizes.
Positive feedback	Give lots of positive feedback! Show honest, sincere appreciation for your students. Be genuine and authentic in your praise.
Go outside	Observing safety considerations, take a break and go outside, and get a breath of fresh air. Have a game or activity prepared and ready to go.

continued on next page

TIPS	EXPLANATION
Keep a routine, avoid surprises	Children like routine and structure, and generally do not deal well with chaos and surprises. Keep choir practices organized and predictable. Have a plan and structure. Write a rehearsal plan on the board. For example, (1) We pray, (2) Vocal warmups and stretches, (3) Song titles to practice, (4) Games, (5) Benediction. Have a child volunteer to check off each item after it's complete. Kids love to help!
Diversify your delivery and teaching methods	Most children have a maximum attention span of around 10 minutes. Don't lecture for long periods. Change up your delivery method to keep it interesting. Show a video, ask the children to write music/songs on the whiteboard, ask them to teach the class a song, etc.
Have the children stand up	Children get antsy and nervous sitting down. Let them stand up while singing and practicing to alleviate tension. Give short breaks to refresh and refocus.
Avoid favoritism	Children are finely tuned to equality and fairness and resent if certain children receive preferential treatment. Be fair to all.
Don't argue with children	Never argue with children. If you become visibly angry or emotional, you will lose credibility with all the children and parents.
Request that sick children stay home	If any kids are sick, they will sneeze and cough on each other and all over the school materials. Request that kids who are sick stay home and follow applicable health and safety protocols.
Choir guidelines and rules	Have a short written rule and policy agreement that the parents read and sign. Then, if a child breaks the rule—for example, consistently misses practice—you can point out that behavior in a fact-based, nonconfrontational way. See the section below on Policies, Rules, and Procedures.

Keep Communicating: Talking, Texting, E-Mailing, Streaming, and Posting to Choir

One of the keys to working well with parents and children is for the choir director to provide a steady stream of text messages, e-mails, web updates, phone calls, and announcements about upcoming activities and events. Additionally, it's a good idea for the choir director to ask the children—multiple times during rehearsals—to repeat, in the child's own words, the date and time for important upcoming events. But even with this plethora of communication by the choir director, parents and children frequently still won't read your e-mails, texts, and announcements, and will miss or be late to critical choir events. Frustrating!

You may have planned a critical rehearsal, only to have just two or three choir members show up for practice. Not surprisingly, at the actual event, children who did not attend practice at all may still appear, unrehearsed, but expecting to sing. In this awkward situation, you may understandably feel like precluding those children who consistently missed practice from singing at the event. On the other hand, you may need them to sing because you are short on children, and so decide to overlook their absences.

Reward Attendance

On the bright side, you will probably be fortunate to have some children who consistently show up at practice and at church each week, prepared and on time. Reward consistent attendance. Put names on an attendance chart in the back of the choir room and have each child put a sticker next to their name for each rehearsal attended. After four rehearsals/performances in a row, give the children a prize. Have a prize box ready with small toys or donations. Send a group e-mail once a week, always on the same day, with the week's planned activities, the upcoming calendar, and any other information parents may need.

Policies, Rules, and Procedures

Misunderstandings and miscommunications between the choir director, children, and parents will inevitably occur, and sometimes, these disagreements can get heated. It is crucial to let parents and children know in advance about the policies, rules, and procedures and the safety considerations that apply to your choir. This will help minimize misunderstandings. Having parents sign some type of a Choir Acknowledgement and Information Form is an excellent way to make clear what are the expectations regarding attendance, special events, fees, materials, safety, etc. If disagreements or misunderstandings later occur with parents or children, you can refer to this signed agreement and show what everyone agreed to. See Appendix C for a sample.

If your children's choir is purely voluntary, free of charge, and/or if your church culture does not support a signed Choir Acknowledgement and Information Form, then as an alternative, a choir director can create a format more along the lines of "Welcome Notes," which provides parents with just the most basic rules and policies for the choir in a more informal form. See Appendix C for a sample e-mail to welcome children/parents to the choir that you can revise and tailor for your needs.

At the very minimum, post a list of "Choir Rules" in the choir room for everyone to see. Have the children help create the rules to give them a sense of ownership in these policies, so that hopefully, they will follow the rules more willingly. Review the rules with the class, discuss the consequences of breaking the rules, and update the rules as needed.

Also, have a vision and a goal for your choir. Consider working with your choir to create a Mission Statement. See Appendix C for a sample Mission Statement that you can modify for your own choir.

CHAPTER 8

Choir Activities Outside of Church

Make a joyful noise to the Lord, all the earth; break forth
into joyous song and sing praises! —Psalm 98:4

One of the things I have found that I love to do is sing and play outside of the church on occasions such as fundraising events, Celebrations of Life, weddings, and other church-related events. When the choir sings in church, it's usually very well orchestrated and planned from a musical perspective. We are usually singing songs that we know well, and we will sing them in the sequence and in the manner that we are accustomed to.

But when the choir sings in places outside of the church, the routine and predictability you are used to can fly out the window. Depending on where the choir is singing, you may be making new music, singing, and playing with singers and musicians you don't really know, wondering what gear and setup are to be used, and overcoming a dozen obstacles and unexpected mishaps. It's exhilarating and refreshing to be outside of your comfort zone singing in a new place and perhaps for different audiences. Below are some of the more common extracurricular church choir events.

Fundraising Events

Churches typically host fundraisers, volunteer activities, and community outreach programs to raise money and advance a cause. Your church needs singing and music at the event to attract people, sell items, receive donations, and be successful. These activities give the choir (or you as an individual) an excellent opportunity to sing and play in a novel setting, outside of the church, and your musical comfort zone. These fundraisers take many forms. A classic example is the church bazaar or equivalent, which is part street fair, concert, and block party. Volunteers set up booths, sell food and used items, hold raffles, take blood pressure, provide all types of entertainment—anything to attract people and raise funds for the church.

Performing and Entertaining

If you have the opportunity, volunteer to sing and play at a fundraising event, as I think you'll really enjoy the experience; I know I have. Here is the fun part: in this situation, set aside everything said in Chapter 4 about not "performing" and not "entertaining." At most fundraisers, you're supposed to entertain and perform; that's the point! So, choose songs that you love to perform, perhaps find another singer to harmonize with you, or add instrumentation, dance if you want, and have fun! If you're nervous about trying to "entertain" people, here's the good news: When you walk on stage and start singing, look out at the audience. Chances are that most of the audience won't be paying attention to you at all. The people will be talking, eating pizza, drinking, walking around, shopping, and so on. Needless to say, you can make all kinds of mistakes, and no one cares or will notice. So, since no one, except your family and friends, is paying you any attention, and since you rarely perform for people, seize the moment, enjoy your time on stage, choose a song you love, do your best, and have fun!

Singing and Playing in the Great Outdoors

You may be accustomed to only singing and playing inside the church in a very controlled environment where all the equipment is set up. Everything is planned and choreographed. But singing and playing outside, under Earth's canopy, is different, with unique challenges such as safety, weather, acoustics, sound systems, technical issues, and such. Think Safety First! Sound equipment carries large voltages and can cause injury or death, so observe all precautions. Don't perform if it's raining or wet, as you could get electrocuted. Also, if you're playing an instrument, don't touch the strings and your mouth to the mic at the same time; you can get a nasty shock or worse. Many singers use a rubber/plastic screen on the mic to reduce the chance of getting shocked. Plus, putting a screen on the mic has the benefit of cutting down wind noise. It's best to use a tarp or perform under an overhead structure for protection against the elements. Below are a few other considerations for singers and musicians playing outside at church events.

Figure 8-1 Being Outdoors, Sunset Cliffs, San Diego, California

Working With a Sound Person

If you perform at one of these fundraisers, and if there is an experienced sound person there, then there should be no need to worry about your sound. As a courtesy, take a few minutes and introduce yourself to the sound person. Let her/him know about your vocal/instrument setup plan, discuss any sound issues or concerns you have, and ask any questions. When you're on stage and getting ready to go, figure out some basic hand cues to communicate with the sound person. For example, if you do a soundcheck, you can point to the monitor and give a thumbs up/thumbs down to indicate if you need the volume to be adjusted up or down.

Doing Your Own Sound

There will be times at church events when you won't have a sound person to mix your sound, and you'll have to do it all yourself. You may need to bring all of your own equipment, including instruments, mics, music stands, cables, amplifiers, monitors, etc. Rather than plugging into a mixing board, you may be plugging directly into your amp and singing directly through the PA speakers. Set up your own monitor so that you can hear yourself. Equipment is discussed generally in Chapter 5, but just a quick a word on mic etiquette: Mics get breathed on, coughed and sneezed on—in short, they are not the most hygienic piece of gear. So, if you can afford it, buy your own mic and keep it with you. You can buy a new Shure SM58, a great mic with cable for a reasonable price.

Use a Monitor

One of the most significant issues for a singer or musician is being able to hear yourself on stage, especially when you are outside, where sound dissipates so quickly. Without a monitor to hear yourself, it's difficult to sound good to the audience. If you are sitting down while singing and playing, you'll need a boom mic stand that adjusts to various positions.

Singing and Playing at a Celebration of Life

Some people may be surprised to learn that many choir members actually enjoy singing and playing at wakes, rosaries, and funerals, often called "Celebrations of Life" occasions where someone has died. But choir members understand that by supporting these events with music, we help those who are hurting, feeling devastated, and in need of comfort. Life and death, sadness, mixed with tributes for the deceased—all merge together in the funeral service. Without music, without songs of hope and faith, a funeral service could become only a sad, somber, and depressing event. But with singing, instruments, and great songs, the choir can transform the mood of the people, help add a feeling of optimism and comfort, and start the beginning of closure.

Richard Diaz, introduced in Chapter 2, says this about his feelings about singing at funerals:

"I love them. The first thing I do when I get to the service is to get a prayer card. I want to know the biographical information, who they were, how old they were, about their family, etc. I sign the guest book, and that way, I feel more connected to the deceased. Often, the family has created a special program, where there are videos, pictures, and testimonials by families and friends about the departed life. It is really hard to sing when the family is so devoted, and when they start crying. When that happens, I try not to look at them, but pick a place at the back of the church to look at, so I don't get too emotional."

Unless a family member or friend asks me to do it, and then I am very honored to do so, I usually avoid playing at funerals for family members or close personal friends. I would rather sit with my family and friends in the pews, watch the service, and grieve with my family. But if the person who died is not family or a close personal friend, then singing and playing at a funeral service is something that I am happy to do. Although it can be very emotional, I enjoy listening and appreciating the life of the person who passed away, as told by the pastor and those who knew the deceased. And when the service is over, I feel a renewed gratitude for my own life, thankful to have more time on the Earth, and more appreciation for my loved ones.

Preparing to Sing at a Funeral

One thing that I always do when I am personally asked to sing and play at a funeral—not as part of the choir but on my own—is that I visit the church, funeral home, or cemetery in advance of the service so that I can become familiar with the location. I like to understand where I will be standing, where the people will be, if I need to bring a mic, PA, and/

or amplifier, set up, and so on. I talk to the pastor in advance to get any helpful tips and suggestions. I also get a copy of the funeral program to understand the sequence of events, when I am supposed to sing, and for how long. The pastor is often extremely experienced regarding the funeral service. I look at the pastor during the service to get visual cues about when to sing and stop.

Remember to expect the unexpected. Things will go wrong, strings will break, sheet music will blow away in the wind (remember to bring clothespins), tablets/computers won't work, and so on. But if you have rehearsed well, memorized at least some of your music, and are over-prepared, then you will overcome these unexpected glitches with poise. Some people may notice that there was a mishap, and they will appreciate that you overcame the issue without missing a beat.

There are hundreds of songs that can be sung and played at Celebrations of Life. See Appendix A for a small sample list. I, along with my sister, Dina, and daughter, Cherie, was recently asked to play at a funeral service for a close family member. It was a great honor to do so, and we were given the discretion to choose whichever songs for the service that we thought would be best. We chose the following songs, many of which were older tunes that seemed to especially fit the service.

SONG	COMPOSER
Safe in the Arms of Jesus	Fanny J. Crosby*
Softly and Tenderly	Will L. Thompson
May the Good Lord Bless and Keep You	Meredith Willson
I know That My Redeemer Lives	Scott Soper
I'll Fly Away	Albert E. Brumley

Read her fascinating story, "Fanny J. Crosby: An Autobiography"

In terms of preparing for a funeral service with a full choir, instead of on my own, our choir practices the songs at least twice, with one of our rehearsals being an hour or two on the day of the funeral, so we are warmed up and ready. Choir attire is white and black. During the funeral service itself, the choir director needs to be watchful and pay careful attention to the cadence of the service—the timing of the eulogy, prayers, communion—so the choir stays in sync with the service. Depending on the number of attendees and the size and length of the service, songs may need to be prolonged or shortened on the spot. Ending the service on time is crucial because often there are additional funeral events scheduled to occur after the service, including greeting mourners, driving via caravan to the cemetery, and allowing time for guests to attend any after-service gatherings.

Figure 8-2 Celebrating Life

Weddings

Weddings can be enjoyable to sing and play at because of the effervescent atmosphere. Love is in the air, and emotions bubble and pop like champagne. I have only played at a couple weddings, but I really enjoyed singing the songs and seeing all the people excited for the bride and groom. If you are friends or family of the wedding party, you already know many of the people coming to the wedding, which means you have a friendly audience. And of course, there is the reception to look forward to!

If you are singing or playing inside a church, the acoustics and audio sound system are often fantastic. You probably won't be singing with a choir but will be singing and/or playing alone or with another person or two. This is helpful because you don't have to worry about a complex arrangement or coordinating with a large choir. Simple and easy. You may need to obtain advance approval from the pastor for the songs that you intend to sing, as many churches require the songs be liturgical in nature.

One infrequent but potentially awkward scenario occurs if the wedding party requests that some relative/friend of the groom or bride sing with you at the ceremony. If you are lucky, this person is a good singer, and after a few rehearsals, he/she is ready to go. If you're not lucky, the person may be vocally challenged and struggle to sing on key and in tempo. In that case, to mitigate the situation, practice as much as you can with them, consider lowering their mic output a bit, so their voice does not overwhelm, sing with them on parts where they are off-key, and try limiting them to one or two songs.

The key to performing well at a wedding is preparation. As discussed in Chapter 3, I tend to over practice in order to be confident, so that I can relax and try and enjoy the experience. An essential item to reduce stress, especially at weddings, funerals, and outside events, is to have a checklist of things you need to bring with you. Make a checklist a few days before the wedding, keep refining it as the day approaches, and then follow it, so you don't forget anything. See Appendix B for my checklist and revise it for your needs.

Fundraising Event for Pets

In case your church is looking for a somewhat different kind of fundraiser, consider having a blessing for animals! Some time back, I noticed one of the local churches was having a "Bless Your Pet Day," where people could bring their pets to the church and have the pastor bless the pet. I had never attended this type of event before. We had a dog named "Rocker" (who has since "gone to glory") so we took him there. There was a huge crowd of people who had brought all types of pets, including dogs, cats, guinea pigs, and birds, to name a few. The pastor took to the podium and talked about how pets were always mentioned and played an essential part in the events of the Bible. And in fact, the pastor continued, when the world was going to be destroyed, Noah was ordered to collect and save the animals in the Ark. The pastor reiterated that there is nowhere in the Bible where it states that pets cannot make it to Heaven.

At the fundraiser, there was a singer, a guitar player, and a simple sound system, which of course made the service that much better. The pastor blessed each pet, and the contribution basket was passed around. From what I could see, this was a very successful event, and I think everyone felt hopeful that their pet had a chance at their eternal reward.

Christmas Caroling

At my church, we have a dedicated group of volunteers who plan and organize Christmas caroling every year. Our "carolers" sing primarily in the homes of our congregation, but they also perform at local res-taurants, shopping malls, retirement homes, anywhere we are invited to sing. Caroling is a fun activity and brings us closer together while spreading the Christmas spirit through music.

A group of church volunteers performs detailed planning to ensure caroling is organized and efficient. As the Christmas season approaches, choir leaders compile a list of Christmas music and lyrics for the songs. Emails are sent out requesting caroling volunteers and providing sched-ule information. We have three separate groups of carolers: One group sings standard American Christmas classics, one group does Hawaii/Island-style Christmas classics, and one group does Filipino/Mexican/American Christmas classics, reflecting the rich ethnic diversity in our area. One thing that I did not realize until I began caroling is the volume of wonderful Christmas music originating from other coun-tries, in different languages, that have such great lyrics and melodies that I had never heard before. Instruments we bring with us include an electric keyboard, ukuleles, flutes, horns, guitars, bass guitars, cajóns, tambourines, etc. Even the humble triangle, neglected and un-chimed since high school, makes a triumphant, tingling appearance.

Our Christmas attire is fun! We wear matching jackets that are custom made for us. Our shirts, pants, and dresses are Christmas col-ors: green, black, and red. The exception is the Hawaii/Island carolers who, of course, wear Hawaiian shirts, leis, and other island accouter-ments. To remind the congregation to invite the carolers to sing at their homes, we perform Christmas songs for the congregation at the end of church service, just as the Christmas season is beginning. We meet on Friday, Saturday, and Sunday nights at the church parking lot. We caravan to our destinations in multiple cars, which is both entertaining and harrowing, as we weave, U-turn, and navigate through streets and freeways to our festive destinations. We may sing at over five homes in one night!

Singing Christmas music is a great bonding experience. It's enjoyable but also a lot of work as it takes significant time expenditure. We don't use an elaborate sound system, and we travel light and nimble. The musicians carry their instruments, amps, and equipment. We've set up everywhere from kitchens to stair landings, backyards, garages, living rooms, and even bathrooms, where the acoustics are unsurpassed. Being a part of the caroling ministry and meeting so many people whom I had never met before, being welcomed into their homes, I've come to realize how much in common we all have with one another. As I enter homes and see the proud family portraits on the wall, smell the food cooking from the kitchen, see the Christmas tree and presents, the family from young to old gathers together to welcome us. It is a reminder that no matter our age, ethnicity, wealth, health, education, or situation, all of us want the best for our family, friends, and ourselves, and strive to do the very best we can.

Singing at Retirement Homes

Singing and playing for senior citizens residing in a retirement home is a truly worthwhile experience. Every December, our Christmas carolers visit one of these facilities. The residents are the best, most enthusiastic, and most appreciative of audiences. The choir is resplendent in Christmas garb. Some retirement homes we have visited have large auditoriums, with stages, and lots of seats for the audience. We typically set up on the stage with singers in front and musicians and amplifiers in the back. The residents seem genuinely excited to hear music. We play our standard Christmas set, and it is rewarding to see how much the audience enjoys it. Music, especially music with a positive message of hope and faith—like Christmas songs—has the power to provide a type of healing, and a positive feeling, especially to people who love music. This is a remarkable gift from any choir to our senior community.

I have to say that being in these retirement homes fills me with many different emotions. I know many seniors are happy and grateful to be living at a quality facility, where they are well cared for. But while many senior citizens are content, even happy, living in these retirement homes, I suspect that many are not and feel lonely and abandoned, no longer living in their own homes even if it was no longer a viable option. So for me, and I suspect for others, singing in retirement homes is a simple way for us to add joy, entertainment, and musical therapy to our seniors. We receive a real feeling of service to others. But accompanying that good feeling is also a hard dose of reality as we catch a glimpse of the final years of so many seniors, and perhaps, we see a preview of our own.

Singing and Playing at Home

Provided that you have space and an accommodating spouse or significant other, the best, most comfortable, and relaxing place to sing and play is in your own home. Everything you need is there—your instruments, sheet music, tablet/computer, amplifiers, mics, music stands, chairs, favorite food, and drink. And if you live in an area with beautiful weather, like I do in Southern California, then the backyard, with all of its beauty and charms, is a wonderful place to play. Almost anytime we have a birthday and other celebrations at my home, we end up singing and playing. We do it informally, casually, without sheet music; we just jam. We take turns, with each person choosing whatever song they want to sing and play. If we all know the song, which we often do, then we all join in. If no one knows the song, then we will all still join in and just fake it 'til we make it.

I am always intrigued at how individual singers and musicians have so much natural talent, instinct, and intuition for music, that they can hear a song for the first time, and then sing an improvised harmony or play an instrumental break on the spot, unrehearsed. Not perfectly, of course, but with style and taste that is so suited to the song. I keep tambourines, shakers, and a cajón handy so that if anyone wants to join in, they can. Our piano is ready in case we are fortunate enough to have a pianist to play with us. To me, the fun and freshness of playing live with your family and friends is one of my best and most cherished musical memories. And of course, I record these jams on my audio/video recorder and listen to them in my car going to work, working on projects in my garage, or working out in the gym. I hope you, too, can find avenues to sing and play, to bring joy to yourself and others, and celebrate life through music.

Acknowledgements

So many people helped and encouraged me as I researched and wrote this book. I especially want to thank those who sat for interviews, corresponded with me via e-mail, text, and telephone, and answered my many questions. These are truly remarkable people who dipped deep into their well of knowledge and experience to share their passions for music, choir, teaching, and faith. They include Arlene Belenzo, Joe Demurs, Bob Diaz, Richard Diaz, Emily Erickson, Dr. John Mark Harris, Shayne McIntyre, Alicia McMillan, Patrick O'Brien, Henry Poblete, Blessie Prudente, Rene Prudente, Dan Quigley, Frances Tuminting, Ric Tuminting, Charles Wilson, and all of my fellow choir members who inspire me with their talent and service.

A huge thank you to Mater Dei Catholic Church. Over twenty years ago, my son, who was fourteen years old, was welcomed into the Mater Dei Church choir, and I joined as well. I'm glad I did, as I discovered the beauty, benefits, and mission of the choir. An added bonus is the friendships that I have made with my fellow choristers. Father Jovencio Ricafort ("Father Ven") is an inspiration. His vision, leadership, and optimism have guided the construction and completion of our beautiful new church, located in Chula Vista, California.

When I asked a friend who worked for many years in the publications field at a large company in San Diego if she could recommend an editor, she said without hesitation, "Tom Hymes is the best." And she was right. Tom is a gifted editor with tremendous focus and editorial discernment. Tom significantly improved the quality of the manuscript, corrected mistakes, and added comments and suggestions that substantially improved its readability.

Tara Mayberry (TeaBerry Creative) created the design and layout of this book and performed the production work needed for publication. Tara created a beautiful design and is a true professional.

I want to thank my mother, Apfinia Hill. She taught me through her example to believe and trust in God, to work hard, and have fun and enjoy each day. Monte Hill is the best father a son could ask for—a Korean War veteran, Golden Gloves boxer, violin player extraordinaire, four-part harmony singer, and the most talented musician I have played with. My sister, Dina, lights up the lives of everyone she knows. She is a supremely dedicated musician—fantastic vocalist and pianist, —and contributed many ideas and suggestions to this book.

I give special thanks to my beautiful wife, Lory, a wonderfully talented artist who painted the images for the cover and produced the other artwork in these pages, including most of the photography. All my love goes to my son, Kenny, and daughter, Cherie, I am so proud of them.

James Hill

Favorite Worship Songs and Hymns

I asked contributors to this book to list some of their favorite worship songs and hymns. Have a listen, and consider adding them to your choir's repertoire (except as otherwise noted). Enjoy!

Alicia McMillan Congregational Hymns:
- Come Thou Fount (words by Robert Robinson, music by John Wyeth)
- Spirit Now Live in Me (Bryan Jeffrey Leach)
- Draw the Welcome Circle Wider (Mary Louise Bringle)
- Go, Be Justice (Martin Willett)
- Bread of the World (Reginald Heber)
- I Come With Joy (Brian A. Wren)
- O Sacred Head, Now Wounded (Bernard of Clairvaux)
- Of the Father's Love Begotten (Aurelius Clemens Prudentius)

Alicia McMillan Children's Anthems:
- Do You Know Your Shepherd's Voice? (Suzanne Lord)

- All songs from Heroes of the Faith (Sacred Children's Musical) (Fred Bock), as arranged by Houston Children's Choir Series
- Houston Children's Choir Series
- Bethlehem Night (Terry Taylor)
- The Snow Lay on the Ground (Vicki Hancock Wright)

Charles Wilson:
- Handel's Messiah (George Frideric Handel)
- Jesu, Joy of Man's Desiring (J.S. Bach)
- Amazing Grace (John Newton)
- How Sweet the Name of Jesus Sounds (John Newton)
- I Want to Be Ready to Walk in Jerusalem Just Like John (author unknown, African-American Spiritual)
- I Love the Lord (Richard Smallwood)
- My Tribute To God Be the Glory (Fanny Crosby), as performed by Andraé Crouch
- Through It All (Andraé Crouch)
- Ordinary People (Danniebelle Hall)
- Yes Lord! (Charles H. Mason: COGIC National Anthem of the Saints of God)
- Majesty (Jack Hayford)
- Praise the Name of Jesus, Praise the Son of God (Jack Hayford)
- Send Judah First (Judith Christie-McAllister)
- Here I Am, Lord (I'm the Lord of Sea and Sky) (Dan Schutte)
- 10,000 Reasons (Bless the Lord O My Soul) (Matt Redman)

Dan Quigley Christian Songs:
- All Creatures (Chad Gardner), as performed by Kings Kaleidoscope

- Sticks & Stones (Zach Bolen, Chad Gardner), as performed by Kings Kaleidoscope
- Benediction (Dan Haseltine, Charlie Lowell, Stephen Mason, Matt Odmark), as performed by Jars of Clay
- I Could Sing of Your Love Forever (Martin Smith), as performed by Delirious?
- Good to Me (Audrey Assad)
- Restless (Audrey Assad)
- Easter Song (Anne Herring), as performed by Keith Green
- Miracle Maker (John Thatcher, Martin Smith, Stuart Garrard, Tim Jupp, Stewart Smith), as performed by Delirious?
- Paint the Town Red (Smith Martin James, John Thatcher, Stuart Garrard, Tim Jupp, Stewart Smith), as performed by Delirious?
- Give Me Your Eyes (Brandon Heath)
- Only Hope (Jonathan Mark Foreman), as performed by Switchfoot
- The Fatal Wound (Jonathan Mark Foreman), as performed by Switchfoot
- Daisy (Jonathan Mark Foreman), as performed by Switchfoot
- Gone (Timothy Foreman, Jonathan Foreman), as performed by Switchfoot
- Crazy Times (Stephen Daniel Mason, Dan Haseltine, Mark Jeffrey Hudson), as performed by Jars of Clay
- Overjoyed (Greg Wells, Mark Hudson, Dan Haseltine, Stephen Mason), as performed by Jars of Clay
- All Is Well (Michael W. Smith and William Kirkpatrick)

Dan Quigley Hymns:
- Let All Mortal Flesh Keep Silence (Gerard Moultrie)
- What Wondrous Love Is This (Samuel Barber)
- All Creatures of Our God and King (William Henry Draper)
- Let All Things Now Living (Katherine K. Davis)
- Alleluia! Sing to Jesus (W. Chatterton Dix)
- Panis Angelicus (Saint Thomas Aquinas)
- Sanctissima (author unknown), as arranged by Fritz Kreisler
- Ave Verum Corpus (Amadeus Mozart)
- Hail Holy Queen (author unknown)
- Ave Maria (Johann S. Bach/Charles Gounod)
- Ave Verum (Philip Stopford)
- Ave Maria (Philip Stopford)
- The Church's One Foundation (Samuel John Stone)
- Great Is Thy Faithfulness (Thomas O. Chisholm)
- Be Thou My Vision (Saint Dallan Forgaill)
- Pange Lingua (Saint Thomas Aquinas)
- Salve Regina (author unknown)
- Lully, Lulla, Lullay (Philip Stopford)
- Now the Green Blade Rises (John Macleod Campbell Crum)
- The Angel Gabriel From Heaven Came (Sabine Baring-Gould)

Dina Hill:
- Because the Lord is My Shepherd (Christopher Walker)
- Canticle of the Sun (Marty Haugen)
- Remember Your Love (Mike Balhoff, Darryl Ducote, Gary Daigle)
- You Are Near (Dan Schutte)
- You Are Mine (David Haus)

- Hail Mary, Gentle Woman (Carey Landry)
- There is Nothing Told (Christopher Willcock)
- Come, Come Emmanuel (Steve Angrisano)
- Behold the Lamb (Martin Willett)
- Though the Mountains May Fall (Dan Schutte)
- Your Grace is Enough (Chris Tomlin)
- I Am the Bread of Life (Sr. Suzanne Toolan)
- Worthy is the Lamb (Ricky Manalo)
- Blest Be the Lord (Dan Schutte)
- On Eagle's Wings (Father Michael Joncas)
- Be Not Afraid (Bob Dufford)
- Turn to Me (John Foley)
- The Servant Song (Richard Gillard)
- In the Day of the Lord (M.D. Ridge)
- The Cry of the Poor (John Foley)

James Hill:
- Down by the Riverside (author unknown, African American spiritual), as performed by Elvis and the Million Dollar Quartet)
- Parable (M.D. Ridge)
- Taste and See (James E. Moore)
- Open My Eyes (Jesse Manibusan). Sing with harmony, especially the bridge
- Ang Katawan ni Kristo, Behold, the Body of Christ (Ricky Manalo, Pia de Leon)
- Two were Bound for Emmaus (Bob Hurd)
- Shall We Gather at the River (Robert Lowry)
- Pan De Vida (Bob Hurd)

- With One Voice (Ricky Manalo)
- Bathed in the Waters of Life (Carey Landry and Carol Jean Kinghorn-Landry)
- I Shall Not Be Moved (Alfred H. and B.D. Ackley), as performed by Elvis and the Million Dollar Quartet
- You've Got to Walk That Lonesome Valley (Woody Guthrie), as performed by Elvis and the Million Dollar Quartet
- With the Lord (Father Michael Joncas)
- Here I Am, Lord (Dan Schutte)
- On Eagle's Wings (Father Michael Joncas)
- To You, O God, I Lift Up My Soul (Bob Hurd)
- Though the Mountains May Fall (Dan Schutte)
- Rise Up With Him (Janet Vogt)
- Healing Waters (Trevor Thomson)
- I'll Fly Away (Albert E. Brumley)
- Will the Circle Be Unbroken (words by Ada R. Habershon, music by Charles H. Gabriel), as performed by the Nitty Gritty Dirt Band, not intended for church services
- Three Wooden Crosses (Doug Johnson and Kim Williams), as performed by Randy Travis, not intended for church services

Dr. John Mark Harris:
- Holy, Holy, Holy! Lord God Almighty (Reginald Heber)
- This Endris Night (author unknown)
- All Creatures of Our God and King (William Henry Draper)
- The King of Love My Shepherd Is (Henry Baker)
- Come, Christians, Join To Sing (Christian H. Bateman)
- It Is Well With My Soul (Horatio Spafford and Philip Bliss)
- Abide With Me (Henry Francis Lyte)

- We Three Kings (John Henry Hopkins Jr.)
- For All The Saints (William Walsham How)
- Prayer of St. Francis (author unknown)

Monte Hill:
- Where We'll Never Grow Old (James Cleveland Moore)
- Family Bible (Willie Nelson), not intended for church services
- The Old Rugged Cross (George Bennard)
- When they Ring Those Golden Bells (Daniele de Marbelle)
- I Come to the Garden Alone (C. Austin Miles)
- Safe in the Arms of Jesus (Fanny J. Crosby)
- Softly and Tenderly (Will L. Thompson)

Christmas Songs:
- Beyond the Moon and Stars (Dan Schutte)
- Soon and Very Soon (Andraé Crouch)
- There Is a Longing (Anne Quigley)
- Come, Come Emmanuel (Steve Angrisano)
- Waiting in Silence (Carey Landry and Carol Jean Kinghorn-Landry)
- Come, All Ye Faithful (John Francis Wade)
- Silent Night (Franz Xaver Gruber and Joseph Mohr)
- By the Star (Janet Vogt)
- Born This Day (Ken Canedo)
- Hark! The Herald Angels Sing (Charles Wesley, George Whitefield)
- Little Town of Bethlehem (Phillips Brooks, Lewis Redner)
- Away in a Manger (*Carl Mueller*)
- Joy to the World (Isaac Watts)

- Come, All Ye Faithful (author unknown)
- Night of Silence (Daniel Kantor)
- Child of the Poor (Scott Soper)
- Angels We Have Heard on High (James Chadwick)
- God Rest You Merry, Gentlemen (author unknown)
- The King Shall Come (Trevor Thomson)
- Holy Night (words Placide Cappeau, music Adolphe Adam)
- What Child is This (words William Chatterton Dix, music Wolfgang Amadeus Mozart)
- The First Noel (author unknown)

Funeral Songs:
- Be Not Afraid (Bob Dufford)
- Shepherd Me, O God (Marty Haugen)
- Blest Are They (David Haas)
- Hail Mary: Gentle Woman (Carey Landry)
- Here I Am, Lord (Dan Schutte)
- We Remember (Marty Haugen)
- Fly Like a Bird (Ken Canedo)
- Parable (M.D. Ridge)
- How Great Thou Art (Carl Boberg)
- I Am the Bread of Life (Sr. Suzanne Toolan)
- On Eagle's Wings (Michael Joncas)
- You Are Mine (David Haas)
- Jesus, Remember Me (Jacques Berthier)
- Like a Shepherd (Bob Dufford)
- Shelter Me, O God (Bob Hurd)
- Soon and Very Soon (Andraé Crouch)
- The Summons (John Bell)

- Taste and See (James E Moore Jr.)
- Let There Be Peace on Earth (Jill Jackson and Sy Miller)
- Softly and Tenderly (Will L. Thompson)
- When They Ring Those Golden Bells (Daniele de Marbelle)
- I'll Fly Away (Albert E. Brumley)
- Song of Farewell (Ernest Sands)

APPENDIX B

Sample Singer/Musician Checklists

SINGER'S ITEMS	MUSICIAN'S ITEMS
□ Show your smile!	□ Show your smile!
□ Mic and cables (if you bring your own microphone)	□ Instrument and case
□ Mic stand (if needed)	□ Amp, mic, cables, and instrument strap (if needed)
□ Tablet/Laptop, (fully charged) with charger, and cleaning cloth	□ Extension cord, three-prong adapter
□ Sheet music	□ Tablet/Laptop, (fully charged) with charger, and cleaning cloth
□ Cell phone (in silent mode) (fully charged) with charger	□ Sheet music
□ Music/Tablet stand (if needed)	□ Mic stand (if needed)
□ Reading glasses	□ Music/Tablet stand (if needed)
□ Pitch pipe	□ Instrument stand
□ Pins/clamps to hold sheet music in place (especially if outside)	□ Extra batteries for instrument, pedals, etc.
□ Tea (throat coat tea), water, throat lozenges (honey), throat spray	□ Capo (for guitar players)
	□ Picks
	□ Rosin (violin players)
	□ Reading glasses
	□ Fingernail clippers
	continued on next page

SINGER'S ITEMS	MUSICIAN'S ITEMS
☐ Gig bag/backpack to hold your stuff ☐ LED light that clamps to music stand for dark settings ☐ Audio recorder with batteries to record choir ☐ Pen/pencil ☐ Mask (if preferred or required) ☐ Small hand sanitizer ☐ Jacket/sweater (in case it's cold) ☐ Tissues or handkerchief ☐ Mask (if preferred or required)	☐ Cell phone (in silent mode) (fully charged) with charger ☐ Tuner ☐ Pedals (if used) ☐ Pins/clamps to hold sheet music open (especially if outside) ☐ Extra strings and string cutter ☐ Tea, water ☐ Gig bag/backpack to hold your stuff ☐ LED light that clamps to music stand for dark settings ☐ Audio recorder with batteries to record choir ☐ Pen/pencil ☐ Mask (if preferred or required) ☐ Small hand sanitizer ☐ Jacket/sweater (in case it's cold) ☐ Tissues or handkerchief
Notes:	Notes:

Children's Choir Supplemental Information

Below is a sample Mission Statement for Children's choir that can be posted to your church's website, in the classroom, etc. Revise and customize this statement for your choir so that everyone shares a common sense of purpose.

- Nurture the spiritual growth of children through music that is based on Scripture.
- Enable children to share in worship and to offer music to the world in the worship of God.
- Make new friends, relieve stress, have fun, and discover the joy of music.
- Serve in the community by singing at retirement centers, church events, and concerts.
- Learn about God in a safe environment where children can express themselves and pray.
- Teach healthy vocal techniques and learn to love to sing.
- Encourage self-expression, creativity, and a love of the arts.

- Experience music through games and movement activities.
- Develop a strong faith and early belief in God and have a positive self image.
- Develop leadership skills, self-confidence, and self-esteem through singing.
- Sing praises to God!

Sample Welcome E-Mail to Parents and Children

Below is a sample e-mail for Children's choir that can be sent to children and parents, welcoming them to the choir. Revise and customize this e-mail in a way that make sense for your choir.

Welcome to our Choir! Here is some information for you:

Calendar:
Please see attached and use for important dates. Please stand by for more information about future rehearsals.

One must attend rehearsal in order to sing at church. It is very important that we give our best to the Lord as ministers of the church. Rehearsal is how we prepare for church.

Attire
Dress appropriately. No jeans, shorts, or flip-flops. We are ministers and should dress appropriately for the Lord.

Reminders for Parents:

Please bring your children ready to serve by having them rested, nourished with food/water, and having already used the restroom. Thank you!

1. Please remember that all children must be accompanied by an adult until choir teachers/directors are there.
2. Parents/Guardians, please sit near the front during the church service to help us in case your child needs you.
3. If your child is sick, please allow him/her to stay home to keep illness from spreading and follow applicable health and safety protocols. Thank you for your consideration.

May our Lord continue to shower His graces upon you and your family!

SAMPLE: Children's Choir Acknowledgement and Information Form

Welcome to _____ Church Choir!
We are blessed and excited that you have chosen to join us!
This acknowledgment is intended to ensure that everyone understands and agrees to choir rules and policies. Please review and discuss this acknowledgement with your child and sign it. If you have any questions or concerns, please see your choir director. Thank you and welcome to the choir!

I. Attendance Requirements

Church Rehearsals and Singing at Church Services
Each member is an integral part of the choir, and we understand that sometimes missing rehearsal is unavoidable. The choir needs to have regular and consistent attendance by all members so that the choir can sound our best. To fully educate and strengthen our children in their faith, and to develop their vocal skills, the choir member agrees to:

- Attend choir rehearsals and sing on your scheduled days in church.
- Notify your choir director of unavoidable absences as soon as possible.
- Avoid tardiness by planning to arrive at all rehearsals and performance calls ten minutes early. Important vocal warm-ups take place at the beginning of each rehearsal.

Musical Productions, Concerts, and Choral Events

Besides singing in church, other fun activities such as concerts, musical productions, concerts, bazaars, Christmas events may be planned during the year. The choir member agrees to:

- Attend rehearsals and participate in scheduled events.
- Attend final rehearsals preceding musical productions and concerts, as those rehearsals are critical for success. The choir director has discretion to revoke performance privileges for choir members who miss too many rehearsals.
- Avoid tardiness by planning to arrive at rehearsals and performance calls ten minutes early. Important vocal warm-ups take place at the beginning of each rehearsal.
- Notify your choir director, preferably by e-mail or text, as soon as possible and let them know if you cannot attend rehearsal or an event.
- If the member continually misses rehearsals, the choir director has discretion to give your spot to another choir member.

2. Take Care of Music and Equipment

The choir member agrees to be responsible for taking care of his/her own music, equipment and instruments. Choir members may be charged the replacement cost of any lost or damaged instrument or equipment.

3. Use of Cell Phones and Devices

Use of cell phones and other devices is not allowed during rehearsals and church services unless needed in emergency situations. Your choir director may give you time during a break in rehearsal to check your phone/device and get up to date on any missed calls or messages.

4. Parent Involvement

The success of any children's program reflects the level of commitment that parents give. Parents are a vital part of this ministry.

- Families are encouraged to attend church services when the choir is singing, and come to concerts and musical productions to support the choir in their musical endeavors. Parents agree to:
- Ensure that each choir member has reliable transportation to and from weekly rehearsals.
- Read all e-mails, text, and announcements from the choir director and respond in a timely fashion.
- Help choir member remember choir policies, rules, announcements, etc.

Parents: We Need Your Help: Please check any of the following areas where you can help the choir:

☐ Costumes
☐ Administrative
☐ Sunday supervision
☐ Sets/props
☐ Robe maintenance
☐ Rehearsal help

5. **Prohibited.** No smoking, alcohol, drugs, or weapons are permitted at practice or performances.

6. **Fees.** Your choir director will let you know if there is a registration fee or other fees.

Choir Member/Parent Agreement

_____

I have read the information contained in the acknowledgement and have reviewed it with my child. We understand the rules and policies contained herein.

By signing below, we agree to follow policies in this acknowledgment.

_____

Signature of choir member   Date

_____

Print choir member name

_____

Signature of parent/guardian   Date

_____

Print parent/guardian name

END

Release of Liability Considerations

Find an experienced attorney and seek advice about including an appropriate Release of Liability/Indemnification Form for participants to sign. This form can help document important items such as participants' consent for various choir activities, provide critical medical/emergency contact information, and help mitigate liability for accidents, medical emergencies, and other unexpected mishaps.

Also, ask the attorney about creating a Publicity Release Form in the event that the news media or others want to post videos or photographs of the choir on TV or social media. Some parents may not want their children to appear on TV or social media, so have the proper notice and consent forms indicated and signed in advance by parents and guardians.

APPENDIX D

Extras

From Chapter 2: The Man Upon the Cross
From Chapter 5: My First Music Teacher

From Chapter 2:

THE MAN UPON THE CROSS
James Hill

Hung a man upon the cross
He was scared, alone, and lost
He knew his sinful life was at an end

He saw Jesus suffering too
And his faith in Jesus grew
He said, remember me when you enter your Kingdom

A JOYFUL CALLING

Chorus
And Jesus said
Today you'll walk with me in Paradise
Leave behind your troubles and your strife
Your sins they are forgiven
And this pain that you've been living
Will fade in the glory of God

I deserve to pay this price
I know I've sinned all my life
I fear God for all the things that I have done
But Jesus, you've done no wrong
And with the soldiers looking on
He said, remember me when you enter your Kingdom

Chorus
Today you'll walk with me in Paradise
Leave behind your troubles and your strife
Your sins they are forgiven
And this pain that you've been living
Will fade in the glory of God

Bridge
Father forgive us, for we know what we do
Father, have mercy when we turn away from you
Grant us peace, grant us peace

Hung a man upon the cross
He was saved, no longer lost
He knew his sinful life was at an end
No longer afraid to die,
And as the sun eclipsed the sky
He knew that his soul was redeemed

Chorus
Today you'll walk with me in Paradise
Leave behind your troubles and your strife
Your sins they are forgiven
And this pain that you've been living
Will fade in the glory of,
Fade in the glory of,
Fade in the glory of God

END

This song will soon be available on Amazon and other sites.

From Chapter 5:

My First Music Teacher

For those of us who took music lessons as a child, we all have our unique memories of our teacher(s) and our experiences learning music, and I am going to recount my memories of my teacher and my first good guitar.

I started my music lessons at about eight years old. My music teacher, Mr. Salerno, had a home, which doubled as his teaching studio, located on University Avenue in San Diego. When I started guitar lessons, I didn't own a guitar, so my father rented a 1950s-era Stella acoustic from Mr. Salerno for ten dollars per month, until we could afford to buy a decent guitar. Even then, and not knowing anything about instruments, I was not proud of this guitar; it seemed to me to be a painted bundle of plywood, devoid of tone, and character. My teacher, on the other hand, played a 1960s sunburst Fender Jazzmaster, which he plugged into a tweed Champ amp, adjusted with the treble turned down—like jazz players do—so that it purred with that warm Fender tone. Mr. Salerno was old, with white hair and scruffy beard, short in stature, and always dressed formally for our lesson, in a white long-sleeve shirt, black pants, and black shoes. I would learn many years later that he had been a professional musician in his younger years, and he and his brothers had played throughout San Diego in various bands and venues.

Mr. Salerno tended to be grumpy and "chewed" me out on numerous occasions for what seemed to me minor musical infractions of time and technique. These included holding my pick incorrectly, tapping my foot out of time, and other musical misdemeanors. As an eight-year-old, I was scared of him.

So, imagine my horror when one day, at home, I dropped and broke his Stella guitar, which, you will recall, we were only renting from him. I was terrified! Since I was already scared of Mr. Salerno, how could I muster the courage to tell him that I had broken his precious guitar, and what would he do about it? I decided to bring in the "big guns," which was my father, himself an accomplished musician. I showed my father the crack in the guitar and the broken bridge, and I was not comforted to see that my father also had a look of concern, no doubt imagining how Mr. Salerno would react to this news. I dreaded my upcoming lesson when I would have to show Mr. Salerno his broken guitar. We took the guitar to a local repair shop, but the repairperson said it was not worth fixing.

When the day of my lesson came, my father walked straight up to Mr. Salerno, who was sitting in his chair, dressed in his usual white shirt and black pants. My father said in a confessional, but bold tone, "Mr. Salerno, *we* broke your guitar!" Mr. Salerno looked stunned for a moment and sat back in his chair, as if he'd received a devastating blow. He recovered himself, and took the guitar in his hands, like a doctor examining a patient who isn't going to survive. He inspected the damage, with a look of restrained irritation. Being smart and thrifty, Mr. Salerno's demeanor changed from doctor to injured businessman, as he considered the remedy. As had been agreed when we rented the Stella, under the rental terms, my father agreed to pay thirty-five dollars to purchase the broken, unplayable, Stella from Salerno, which was much more than it was worth and a lot of money to my father in those days. We now had to shop for me to buy another guitar.

My First Good Guitar

For every door that closes, another one opens. For me, the devastation of the Stella, though unnerving at the time, led me to acquire a fabulous instrument that I never could have dreamed of. My father took me to a used music store to look for a replacement guitar. As soon as we walked in, I spied a candy-apple red, semi-acoustic Harmony, with F holes—a Chuck Berry electric-style guitar. It was everything I wanted before I knew I wanted it, and it was love at first sight. I don't think I had ever held an electric guitar before, and I could feel its potential power when I plugged it into the amp and played it. My father purchased the Harmony for $120.00 including a case and little amp. It was a financial stretch for my father, and he had to finance the purchase and make payments over time to the store. But the next week I walked into my guitar lesson, as proud as I could be, even a little embarrassed, of my new guitar, and my meteoric rise in guitar status. Mr. Salerno inspected it, played it, asked how much we paid, and nodded his head approvingly, saying that this was a very good guitar. I loved to play that Harmony, enjoyed practicing on it, and because it was an inspiring guitar to play, I improved.

In time, Mr. Salerno actually looked forward to our lessons, and enjoyed playing the guitar duets, from the Mel Bay books that we played together, and the "chew" faded away. Sometimes when we were playing really well together, he would close his eyes, recline back in his chair, his fingers moving along the Jazzmaster fret board, the Fender Champ amp purring with music. In those musical moments, our differences in age and temperament, along with any sore feelings, faded away, and we were both friends in music.

In hindsight, I am so grateful Mr. Salerno was my teacher. He was strict with me on time, technique, and reading music. And now I understand that he was right to be strict. He was strict because he cared so much about music; it was his passion and his life's vocation, and he wanted music to be learned and played correctly with discipline. Even the Stella, once a source of pain and embarrassment to me, has become an old friend, a tangible memory of a time long past, that is now fading rapidly from view. My Stella hangs on the wall of my home, soon to be repaired and restored to its former glory by my son, Kenny.

Figure D-1 Harmony and Stella Guitars

Lightning Source UK Ltd.
Milton Keynes UK
UKHW021258081122
411855UK00025B/424